D1314077

INTRODUCTION

The *Checkmate Pocket Guide*, in its third edition, will help you find quick answers to questions about writing style, grammar, and documentation. This guide is pocket-sized to make it easy to carry around as a handy reference book.

Although compact, *Checkmate* is broad in its coverage and includes a wealth of information about grammar, writing style, punctuation, and mechanics, such as capitalization, abbreviation, and spelling. This guide provides easy access to the complexities of documentation styles, including, in this new edition, Institute of Electrical and Electronics Engineers citation style along with the styles of the Council of Science Editors, the Modern Language Association, the American Psychological Association, Columbia Online Style, and *The Chicago Manual of Style*. Sample notes and bibliographical entries, as well as sample pages from student research essays, give you models for formatting title pages, text, notes, and references.

Examples are the key to clarity in understanding how to write and format academic material. This guide provides a clear table of contents, illustrations of errors and their correction, text boxes with pertinent examples, and a glossary of usage for easy reference.

Checkmate Pocket Guide, a short, portable, but comprehensive style guide, will help students find answers to questions about accepted conventions of writing, throughout college and university and in their professional careers.

Joanne Buckley

THIRD EDITION

Checkmate

Pocket Guide

Joanne Buckley
with technical updates by
Cassandra Alexopoulos

NELSON / EDUCATION

NELSON / EDUCATION

Checkmate Pocket Guide, Third Edition

by Joanne Buckley, with technical updates by
Cassandra Alexopoulos

**Vice President, Editorial
Higher Education**
Anne Williams

Executive Editor:
Laura Macleod

Senior Marketing Manager:
Amanda Henry

Developmental Editor:
Caron Macmenamin

Permissions Coordinator:
Debbie Yea

**Content Production
Manager:**
Claire Horsnell

Copy Editor:
Sheila Wawanash

Proofreader:
Elizabeth Phinney

Indexer:
Edwin Durbin

**Senior Production
Coordinator:**
Ferial Suleman

Design Director:
Ken Phipps

Managing Designer:
Franca Amore

Interior Design:
Katherine Strain

Cover Design:
Greg Devitt

Compositor:
Carol Magee

Printer:
R.R. Donnelley

Library and Archives Canada
Cataloguing in Publication
Data

Buckley, Joanne, 1953–
Checkmate pocket guide /
Joanne Buckley. — 3rd ed.

Includes index.
ISBN 978-0-17-650850-0

1. English language—Rhetor
—Handbooks, manuals, etc.
2. English language—Gramm
—Handbooks, manuals, etc.
3. Report writing—Handboo
manuals, etc. I. Title.

PE1408.B8185 2012
 808′.042
C2011-907585-7

ISBN-13: 978-0-17-650850-0
ISBN-10: 0-17-650850-3

CREDITS

Chapter 3, p. 88: Reprinted from "The Hidden Room" (in two volumes) by P.K. Page by permission of
the Porcupine's Quill. Copyright (c) P.K. Page, 1997.

Chapter 4, p. 103: By William Carlos Williams, from *The Collected Poems: Volume 1, 1909–1939*,
copyright © 1938 by New Directions Publishing Corp. Reprinted by permission of New Directions
Publishing Corp.

Chapter 5, p. 117: "Civil Elegies" from *Civil Elegies and Other Poems*. Copyright © 1972 by Dennis Le
Reproduced with the permission of House of Anansi Press, Toronto.

GRAMMAR
grammar

GRAMMAR

Common Sentence Errors

The following sections catalogue a number of common errors made by writers in English. Use these sections to revise your work and to respond to questions and suggestions about your use of language. If you discover that you have a tendency to make any one of these errors with some frequency, review the relevant section carefully to internalize the information you find. Doing so will improve your sense of grammar for the next piece of writing you complete. Current grammar checkers are mainly quite reliable, but it is still up to you to accept or reject the changes suggested, and to understand them. The grammar in this chapter reflects formal usage in business and academic documents, but usage is key: e-mail and instant messaging have created increasingly informal usage. Be aware of the level of formality you need in a given document.

Sentence Fragments

A sentence is, at the very least, one complete independent clause that contains a subject and verb. A **sentence fragment**, on the other hand, is part of a sentence that is set off as if it were a whole sentence by a beginning capital letter and a final period or other end punctuation. However, the fragment lacks essential requirements of a grammatically complete and correct sentence.

For example, the fragment may lack a main verb.

Just Phil and I.

A sentence fragment may lack a subject.

Pacing the hallway.

Note that even a phrase such as "Just Phil and I, pacing the hallway" does not have a main verb. Don't confuse the participle *pacing* with a main verb. Here the participle operates as an adjective and modifies "Phil and I"; it doesn't provide a main action for the sentence.

A sentence fragment could also be a subordinate clause commencing with a subordinating word.

When I fly a kite.

Sentence fragments give readers a fragment of a thought as opposed to a complete thought, and they interfere with writing clarity. In any type of academic writing, sentence fragments are considered a serious writing error, and they must be eliminated.

TESTING FOR SENTENCE FRAGMENTS

Fragments can be spotted easily when they appear in isolation, but they are more difficult to identify when they are near complete sentences. If you suspect a group of words is a sentence fragment, consider the following:

1. Does the word group have a verb?
   - ❑ YES. Consider the next question.
   - ❑ NO.   *The word group is a fragment and must be revised to include a verb.*

2. Does the word group have a subject?
   - ❑ YES. Consider the next question.
   - ❑ NO.   *The word group is a fragment and must be revised to include a subject.*

3. Does the word group start with a subordinating word, making it a subordinate clause?
   - ❑ YES. *The word group is a sentence fragment and must be revised to create a complete sentence that is an independent clause.*
   - ❑ NO.   If you answered yes to the two previous questions and no to this one, the word group is a complete sentence and does not require revision for sentence completeness.

Make sure to consider all three questions when reviewing your sentence since a fragment could be missing more than one essential sentence element. If your evaluation indicates that you have a sentence fragment, use the following strategies to transform it into a complete sentence.

ELIMINATING SENTENCE FRAGMENTS

To fix the sentence fragment and make it a complete sentence, do one of the following:

1. Attach the sentence fragments to an independent clause or a clause that contains the essential element lacking in the fragment (e.g., a subject or a verb).

   Just Phil and I <u>were pacing</u> the hallway.

2. Compose an independent clause from the fragment.

   At the emergency ward, <u>the parents were</u> pacing the hallway.

3. Drop the subordinating word.

   ~~When~~ I fly a kite.

SUBORDINATE CLAUSES

A subordinate clause contains a subject and a predicate, or verb, but the clause begins with a subordinating word or phrase (e.g., *after, although, if, until*) or a relative pronoun (*that, which, what, who*). Therefore, the clause is not independent.

You can make a subordinate clause into an independent clause in one of two ways.

1. Merge the subordinate clause with a nearby sentence.

    Many of Elmore Leonard's novels have been made into

    movies, ~~Because~~ because he is an amazingly popular crime writer.

2. Delete the subordinating element of the clause.

    Many of Elmore Leonard's novels have been made into

    movies. ~~Because~~ He is an amazingly popular crime writer.

PHRASES

A phrase is a group of words that does not have either a subject or a verb, and, therefore, cannot stand alone as an independent clause or sentence. Look at these examples:

> to go kayaking

> for the umpteenth time

> with great trepidation

Major types of phrases include noun phrases, adjective phrases, adverb phrases, and prepositional phrases.

FIXING PHRASE FRAGMENTS
You can address phrase fragment problems in two ways.

1. Incorporate the phrase into a nearby sentence.

    Our community library has an amazing array of resources, which is there for ~~For~~ every local citizen to use.

    The phrase *for every local citizen to use* has been added to the sentence in a subordinate clause.

    He took part in the smudging, a ~~A~~ ceremony that uses smoke to purify the psychic energy field, or aura, around a person.

    The writer has used the phrase beginning *a ceremony that uses smoke* as an appositive to rename *smudging*.

2. Turn the phrase into a complete sentence by adding a subject, predicate (verb), or both.

Smokejumpers land with heavy gear, including two parachutes, puncture-proof Kevlar suits, freeze-dried food, fire shelters, and personal effects.

Next, ~~cardboard boxes~~ *containing* ~~heaved out of the airplane~~ chain saws, shovels,

and axes *are heaved out of the airplane*.

Cardboard boxes has become the subject, and the verb has been changed to *are heaved*.

OTHER WORD GROUPS

Other commonly fragmented word groups include

- compound predicates
- examples introduced by *for example*, *such as*, and *for instance*
- lists

The following section will help you identify these fragmentation problems and provides strategies for correcting them.

COMPOUND PREDICATES

The predicate is the part of the sentence that contains the verb. It indicates what the subject is doing or experiencing, or what is being done to the subject. A **compound predicate** contains two or more predicates with the same subject.

Joel wanted to buy a new computer and printer. ~~But~~ *but* could afford to purchase only a used laptop.

The fragment starting *But could* has been made part of the compound predicate. Note that no comma is required between compound elements of this predicate.

EXAMPLES INTRODUCED BY **FOR EXAMPLE, SUCH AS,** AND **FOR INSTANCE**

Often you will need to introduce examples, illustrations, and explanations to support arguments and ideas in your academic writing. Some common words and phrases used to introduce examples, illustrations, and explanations include the following:

also, and, as an illustration, besides, but, equally important, especially, for example, for instance, furthermore, in addition, in particular, including, like, mainly, namely, or, specifically, such as, that is, to illustrate

Sometimes a fragment introduced by any one of the above words or phrases can be attached to the sentence before it to create a complete sentence.

Any treatment of early-seventeenth-century English literature

must include a discussion of the period's leading figures. ~~Such~~ *Such* as John Donne, Ben Jonson, and John Milton.

However, in some instances you may find it necessary to change the fragment containing the examples into a new sentence.

Jan Morris's travel pieces cover many interesting cities. For

instance, ~~exploring~~ *she explores* Beirut, ~~visiting~~ *visits* Chicago, and ~~discovering~~ *discovers* "The Navel City" of Cuzco.

The writer corrected the fragment beginning *For instance* by adding the subject *she*, creating a complete sentence.

FRAGMENTS IN LISTS
Occasionally, list elements are fragmented. This type of writing problem can usually be corrected through the use of a colon or dash.

During my rare vacations, I work on my three R's. ~~Reading,~~ *: reading* relaxing, and running.

ACCEPTABLE FRAGMENTS

Professional writers may use sentence fragments intentionally for emphasis or effect.

Creating Emphasis
A strange place it was, that place where the world began. A place of incredible happenings, splendours and revelations, despairs like multitudinous pits of isolated hells. A place of shadow-spookiness, inhabited by the unknowable dead. A place of jubilation and of mourning, horrible and beautiful.
    —*Margaret Laurence, "Where the World Began" in* Heart of a Stranger *(Toronto: McClelland & Stewart, 1976).*

Making Transitions
Now for the con side.

In Exclamations
Not bloody likely!

Answering Questions
And should we go along with this position? Under no circumstances.

Advertising
Proven effective.

Many instructors do not accept sentence fragments, even intentional ones, in formal writing. Fragments may be acceptable in less-formal writing contexts, such as an informal personal essay or an article for a campus newspaper. Even in contexts where they are permitted, do not overuse sentence fragments.

Comma Splices and Fused Sentences

Incorrectly joining two or more independent clauses within a sentence is a common writing error. An independent (or main) clause contains at least a subject and a verb, and the clause can stand on its own as a separate grammatical unit. When two independent clauses appear in a single sentence, they must be joined in one of two ways:

1. using a comma and one of the seven coordinating conjunctions (*and, but, for, nor, or, so, yet*)
2. with a semicolon or other acceptable punctuation such as a dash or a colon

Fused sentences (also known as run-on sentences) or **comma splices** occur when two independent clauses are incorrectly joined within the same sentence.

FUSED SENTENCES
In a fused sentence, no punctuation or coordinating conjunction appears between the two independent clauses (IC).

     IC   *IC*
✗ Canada's most famous racing ship is the *Bluenose* it was primarily designed to fish the Atlantic coast.

The first independent clause in this fused sentence is *Canada's most famous racing ship is the* Bluenose. The second independent clause is *it was primarily designed to fish the Atlantic coast.*

COMMA SPLICES
In a sentence that contains a comma splice, the independent clauses are joined (or spliced) with commas and no coordinating conjunction.

✗ Canada's most famous racing ship is the *Bluenose*, it was primarily designed to fish the Atlantic coast.

Often writers use conjunctive adverbs in place of coordinating conjunctions and, in doing so, create comma splice errors. A coordinating conjunction is one of these seven words: *and, but, for, nor, or, so,* and *yet*. A conjunctive adverb, on the other hand, is a word such as *furthermore, however,* or *moreover*. However, merely placing the word *however* and commas between the two independent clauses does not correct a comma splice error.

Comma Splice Involving Conjunctive Adverb
✗ Canada's most famous racing ship is the *Bluenose*, however, it was primarily designed to fish the Atlantic coast.

IDENTIFYING FUSED SENTENCES OR COMMA SPLICES IN YOUR WRITING

Use the following checklist to determine if a sentence is fused or is a comma splice.

- The sentence contains two independent clauses.
  - ❑ NO.   Neither of the errors applies.
  - ❑ YES.   Proceed to the next question.
- The independent clauses are joined by a comma and a coordinating conjunction.
  - ❑ YES.   The clauses are correctly joined.
  - ❑ NO.   Proceed to the next question.
- The independent clauses are joined by a semicolon or other acceptable punctuation, such as a colon or a dash.
  - ❑ YES.   The clauses are correctly joined.
  - ❑ NO.   *Use one of the revision strategies provided in the next section to correct the fused sentence or comma splice.*

STRATEGIES FOR CORRECTING FUSED SENTENCES OR COMMA SPLICES

You have four major options for correcting fused sentences or comma splices.

1. Add a comma and a coordinating conjunction (*and, but, for, nor, or, so, yet*)

   Canada's most famous racing ship is the *Bluenose*, yet it was primarily designed to fish the Atlantic coast.

2. Add a semicolon or other appropriate punctuation, such as a colon or a dash.

   Canada's most famous racing ship is the *Bluenose*; it was primarily designed to fish the Atlantic coast.

OR

Canada's most famous racing ship is the *Bluenose*; <u>however</u>, it was primarily designed to fish the Atlantic coast.

3. Revise the sentence to subordinate one of the clauses.

   <u>Even though</u> Canada's most famous racing ship is the *Bluenose*, it was primarily designed to fish the Atlantic coast.

4. Turn each independent clause into a separate complete sentence.

   Canada's most famous racing ship is the *Bluenose*. <u>It</u> was primarily designed to fish the Atlantic coast.

REVISION WITH COORDINATING CONJUNCTION

A comma must precede the coordinating conjunction (*and, but, for, nor, or, so, yet*).

It was minus 30 degrees with a wind chill factor ˄ I still had to walk my dogs.

, but

Mordecai Richler was a fine novelist, ˄ he was also an amusing essayist.

and

REVISION WITH SEMICOLON OR COLON

Use a semicolon without a conjunction if the relationship between the two independent clauses is very clear.

The results of the chemistry experiment were disappointing; our attempt to turn salad dressing into fine cognac had failed miserably.

Use a semicolon and a comma with independent clauses that are joined with a conjunctive adverb or transitional phrase, such as the following:

also, as a result, besides, consequently, conversely, for example, for instance, furthermore, in addition, in fact, meanwhile, moreover, nonetheless, next, on the other hand, otherwise, similarly, subsequently, then, therefore, thus

Margaret Atwood is Canada's foremost living novelist; <u>furthermore</u>, she is among our leading poets.

Use a colon if the first independent clause introduces the second.

The requests are thorough and varied: a chicken or rabbit will be skinned, boned, quartered, shredded, turned into patties, prepared for stew, the liver for this, the kidney for that.

REVISION BY SUBORDINATING SENTENCES

This option for correcting fused sentence and comma splices is usually the most effective, since it provides the most revision choices. You will first need to decide which of the independent clauses you would like to emphasize.

When the
~~The~~ family visited Niagara Falls^, we enjoyed visiting the wax museum, playing mini-golf,^ and taking pictures of the falls.

that
The rules of hockey developed in the 1870s~~, they~~ stipulated ^ there be nine players on a team instead of six as there are today.

Since there
~~There~~ is a smog alert in south-central Ontario, people with breathing difficulties are not supposed to go outside.

REVISION BY RESTRUCTURING

Since the clauses in fused sentences and comma splices are independent, they can stand on their own as separate grammatical units.

. These
Those who run for office are required to speak~~, the~~ speeches must be no longer than five minutes in length.

. The
There is one council member from each region ^ ~~the~~ chairperson is elected by the council members.

Problems with Pronouns

A pronoun is a word that replaces a noun or another pronoun. Three major types of pronoun problems occur frequently in writing:

1. *Antecedent agreement problems:* The pronoun does not agree with the noun or pronoun to which it refers.
2. *Reference problems:* It is not clear to which noun or pronoun the pronoun refers.

3. *Case problems:* The case of a pronoun is its form in a particular sentence context—whether the pronoun functions as a
subject, object, or possessive. Writers sometimes confuse
pronoun case. Two common pronoun case difficulties
involve the following:
   a) when to use *I* instead of *me*, *he* instead of *him*, *they*
      instead of *them*, and so on (that is, the subjective and
      objective cases of personal pronouns)
   b) when to use *who* instead of *whom*

The following four sections provide guidance in identifying,
avoiding, and—if necessary—correcting these types of pronoun
errors.

PRONOUN–ANTECEDENT AGREEMENT

The antecedent is the word the pronoun replaces. (*Ante* in
Latin means *before*.) A pronoun must agree with its antecedent.
   If the antecedent is singular, the pronoun that refers to it
must also be singular.

The <u>microbiologist</u> adjusted <u>his</u> microscope.

Similarly, if the antecedent is plural, the pronoun must be
plural.

The choir <u>members</u> opened <u>their</u> song books.

MAKING PRONOUNS AGREE WITH ANTECEDENTS THAT ARE INDEFINITE PRONOUNS

Indefinite pronouns do not refer to any specific person, thing,
or idea:

   another, anybody, anyone, anything, each, either, every-
   body, everyone, everything, neither, no one, nobody, none,
   nothing, one, somebody, someone, something

In formal English, treat indefinite pronouns as singular even
though they may seem to have plural meanings.

his or her

<u>Anyone</u> who knows the answer should enter it using ~~their~~
keyboard.

CORRECTING INDEFINITE-PRONOUN AGREEMENT PROBLEMS

Often when you are editing a piece of writing, you may find
that you have used a plural pronoun to refer to a singular

indefinite pronoun. In such instances, you might apply the follow strategies for correcting the pronoun agreement problem.

1. Change the plural pronoun to a singular, such as *he* or *she*.

   When the airplane hit severe turbulence, everyone feared for ~~their~~ *his or her* safety.

2. Make the pronoun's antecedent plural.

   When the airplane hit severe turbulence, ~~everyone~~ *the passengers* feared for their safety.

3. Recast the sentence to eliminate the pronoun agreement problem.

   When the airplane hit severe turbulence, ~~everyone feared for their safety~~ *safety was a common fear among all those on board*.

Since the use of *his* or *her* can be awkward and wordy, especially if used repeatedly, you might consider correction strategies 2 and 3 as preferable alternatives. However, be careful to use inclusive language when gender is involved.

GENERIC NOUNS

A **generic noun** names a typical member of a group, such as a typical *classroom teacher*, or a typical *dentist*. Generic nouns might appear to be plural; however, they are singular.

Each Olympic <u>athlete</u> must sacrifice if <u>he or she plans</u> [not *they plan*] to win a gold medal.

If a plural pronoun incorrectly refers to a generic noun, there are three major ways to remedy the error. As you will notice, they are the same as those outlined above for correcting indefinite-pronoun agreement problems.

Although the average Canadian complains about overwork, ~~they feel~~ *he or she feels* powerless to cut back.

Although ~~the average Canadian complains~~ *Canadians complain* about overwork, they feel powerless to cut back.

The   *but feels*
~~While the~~ average Canadian complains about overwork, ~~they feel~~ powerless to cut back.

COLLECTIVE NOUNS

A collective noun names a group of people or things. Examples of collective nouns include *audience, army, choir, class, committee, couple, crowd, faculty, family, group, jury, majority, number, pack,* and *team.*

IF THE COLLECTIVE NOUN REFERS TO A UNIT
Use the singular pronoun.

The <u>audience</u> stood and applauded to show <u>its</u> approval.

IF PARTS OF THE COLLECTIVE NOUN ACT INDIVIDUALLY
Use a plural pronoun.

The <u>audience</u> folded up <u>their</u> lawn chairs and left the park.

Often it is a good idea to emphasize that the antecedent is plural by adding a word, such as *members*, describing individuals within the group.

The audience <u>members</u> folded up <u>their</u> lawn chairs and left the park.

MAINTAIN SINGULAR OR PLURAL CONSISTENCY
Whether you treat the collective noun as singular or plural, ensure that you consistently treat references within the sentence as singular or plural respectively.

has
The faculty ~~have~~ completed its review of courses for the upcoming term.

Its is a singular pronoun but *have* is a plural verb form. To be consistent, the verb should be changed to *has.* The sentence could also be revised to read: *The faculty have completed their review of courses for the upcoming term,* but in that case it might be preferable to add the word *members* after *faculty.*

COMPOUND ANTECEDENTS

TWO OR MORE ANTECEDENTS JOINED BY AND
Antecedents joined by *and* form a **compound antecedent** and require a plural pronoun whether the antecedents are plural or singular.

Dave and Michaela were hungry after their [not *his and her*] day of skiing in Whistler.

TWO OR MORE ANTECEDENTS CONNECTED BY OR, NOR, EITHER . . . OR, NEITHER . . . NOR
Make the pronoun agree with the nearest antecedent.

Either Melodie or the Chans will have their way.

Note: With a compound antecedent such as the one above, place the plural noun last to prevent the sentence from sounding awkward.

Neither the captain nor the other players could explain their lopsided defeat.

In a sentence with a compound antecedent in which one antecedent is masculine and the other is feminine, rewrite the sentence to avoid any gender problem.

Original: Either Michelle or Yuri will be selected to have his documentary previewed at the campus film festival.

Rewrite: The judges will select Michelle's or Yuri's documentary for a preview at the campus film festival.

PRONOUN REFERENCE

A pronoun is a word that replaces a noun or another pronoun. Using pronouns allows you to avoid repeating nouns in speech and writing.

Once Jarod made the sandwich, he packed it in a brown bag.

The noun or pronoun that the pronoun replaces is its antecedent. Here the pronoun *he* clearly relates to the antecedent *Jarod*, and the pronoun *it* clearly relates to the antecedent *sandwich*.

However, when the relationship between the antecedent and the pronoun is ambiguous, implied, vague, or indefinite, the intended meaning can become unclear or completely lost to the reader.

AVOIDING AMBIGUITY ABOUT PRONOUN REFERENCE
When it is possible for a pronoun to refer to either one of two antecedents, the sentence is ambiguous.

Ambiguous: <u>Franz</u> told <u>his</u> <u>father</u> that <u>his</u> car needed a new transmission.

[arrows labeled 1 and 2 above the sentence]

In this sentence the second possessive pronoun *his* could refer to *Franz* or *his father:* is Franz talking about his father's car or his own car?

To eliminate the ambiguity, either repeat the clarifying antecedent or rewrite the sentence.

Option 1: Franz told his father that his father's car needed a new transmission.

Option 2: Franz said, "Dad, your car needs a new transmission."

AVOIDING IMPLIED ANTECEDENTS

The reader should be able to clearly understand the noun antecedent of any pronoun. This antecedent must be stated and not implied or merely suggested.

Before the raging fire spread too close to nearby farms, ~~they~~ the residents were ordered to leave their homes.

Although in the original sentence it is implied that the occupants of the farms were the ones ordered to leave, it is not explicitly stated. The pronoun *they* has no clear antecedent.

Ensure that antecedents refer to nouns present in, or near, the sentence.

In ~~Naomi Wolf's~~ Naomi Wolf *The Beauty Myth,* ~~she~~ explores the relationship between gender and work.

In the original sentence, the construction is redundant and ungrammatical. A pronoun cannot refer to a possessive form, just to a noun.

AVOIDING VAGUENESS WHEN USING PRONOUNS

Pronouns such as *this, that, which,* and *it* should refer clearly to a specific noun antecedent and not large groups of words expressing ideas or situations.

The international figure skating organization agreed to a major overhaul of the judging process; however, ~~it~~ the change took time.

A spot forecast may state that a temperature range for a specific canyon in the forest will be between 25 and 30 degrees; the humidity between 12 and 14 percent, and the

winds 15 kilometres an hour. ~~This interests~~ All of these details interest firefighters.

AVOIDING INDEFINITE USE OF *IT*, *THEY*, OR *YOU*

The pronouns *it*, *they*, and *you* must have clear, definite antecedents.

USING IT

Do not use the pronoun *it* indefinitely (e.g., "In this book it says . . .").

~~In~~ Chapter 23 of the textbook ~~it~~ states that one of the most important factors in transforming Canadian culture was the change in immigration patterns.

USING THEY

Never use *they* without a definite antecedent.

In a typical Hollywood movie, ~~they~~ the director, screenwriter(s), and actors manipulate the audience's emotions.

USING YOU

In formal writing, the use of *you* is acceptable when you are addressing the reader directly.

If <u>you</u> do not want the beeper on, select OFF, and if <u>you</u> want it loud, select HIGH.

In formal writing, do not use *you* as an indefinite pronoun.

In ancient Greece ~~you~~ one dropped a mussel shell into a certain jar to indicate that a defendant was guilty.

PRONOUN CASE (*I* VS. *ME*, ETC.)

Case refers to the form a pronoun takes according the function of that pronoun in a sentence. In English there are three cases.

1. The **subjective case** indicates that the pronoun functions as a subject or a subject complement.
2. The **objective case** indicates that the pronoun functions as the object of a preposition or a verb.
3. The **possessive case** indicates that the pronoun shows ownership.

PRONOUN CASES		
SUBJECTIVE	OBJECTIVE	POSSESSIVE
I	me	my, mine
we	us	our, ours
you	you	your, yours
she/he/it	her/him/it	her/his/its, hers
they	them	their, theirs

The remainder of this section will help you to clearly distinguish between the subjective and the objective case; it also explains how to avoid common pronoun case errors. The final part of the section explains common uses of pronouns in the possessive case.

SUBJECTIVE CASE

The subjective case (*I, we, you, she/he/it, they*) must be used when the pronoun functions as a subject or as a subject complement.

As a Subject
<u>Tony and I</u> split the cost of the video.

A subject complement is a noun or adjective that follows a linking verb and renames or describes the sentence subject. Since the way pronouns are used in the subjective case often sounds quite different from the way you might use pronouns in informal speech, subjective case pronouns as subject complements frequently cause writing difficulties.

As a Subject Complement

The students who did the most work are Ivan and ~~her~~ *she*.

In all formal writing, ensure that you use the subjective pronoun case when the pronoun is part of the subjective complement.

The <u>woman</u> Anatole married is <u>she</u>.

The subject complement of the subject *woman* is the pronoun *she*.
If the construction sounds too unnatural, you may wish to recast the sentence.

<u>She</u> is the <u>woman</u> Anatole married.

OBJECTIVE CASE

An objective case pronoun (*me, us, you, her/him/it, them*) is used when the pronoun functions in any of the following ways:

- as a direct object

  The instructor asked <u>her</u> to read the poem.

- as an indirect object

  The invigilator gave pencils to Sam, Duncan, and <u>me</u>.

- as the object of a preposition

  Just between you and <u>me</u>, the Russian's routine was superior.

IN COMPOUND SUBJECTS AND OBJECTS

A compound subject or a **compound object** includes more than one pronoun.

COMPOUND SUBJECT

<u>She and I</u> went to the multiplex to see a movie.

COMPOUND OBJECT

The park proposal surprised <u>her and me</u>.

The fact that the subject or object is compound does not affect the case of the pronoun. However, compound structures often cause writers to confuse pronoun case.

To determine if you have selected the correct pronoun case, try mentally blocking out the compound structure and focusing on the pronoun in question. Then, decide if the pronoun case you have selected is correct.

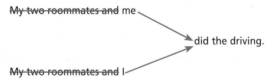

You would say *I did the driving* so the correct choice for the compound is *My two roommates and I did the driving.*

> *I*
>
> In spite of our difficulties, my uncle and ~~me~~ had a wonderful vacation in Mexico.

You wouldn't say *me had a wonderful vacation*, so the correct choice is *my uncle and I*. The pronoun is part of the subject of the sentence, so the subjective case is required.

> *me*
>
> After the class, the librarian gave detentions to Rachel and ~~I~~.

You wouldn't say *gave detentions to I,* so the correct choice is *to Rachel and me.* The pronoun is the indirect object, so the objective case is required.

Resist the impulse to use a reflexive pronoun such as *myself* or *himself* when you are uncertain about the pronoun case.

> *me*
>
> The contest organizers sent the entry forms to Del and ~~myself~~.

In this sentence, *Del and me* are the indirect objects of the verb *sent,* so the objective case (*me*) is correct.

AS APPOSITIVES

An appositive is a noun or noun phrase that renames a noun, noun phrase, or pronoun. When a pronoun functions as an appositive, it has the same function, and hence the same case, as the noun or pronoun it renames.

> Three members of the debating team—Clara, Michael, and
> *I*
> ~~me~~—were mentioned in the article.

Clara, Michael, and I is an appositive for the sentence subject *three members.* As a result, the subjective case of the pronoun is required.

> *me*
>
> Let's you and ~~I~~ take the weekend off and go to the St. Jacob's market.

You and me is an appositive to *us* (*let's* is a contraction of *let us*). *Us* is the objective of the verb *let;* therefore, the objective case of the pronoun is required.

WHEN **WE** OR **US** PRECEDES A NOUN

Sometimes you may need to decide whether *we* or *us* should come before a noun or noun phrase. Mentally block out the noun so that only the pronoun remains. Then, decide which pronoun case is correct.

We ~~piano players~~

play scales every day.

Us ~~piano players~~

We is correct since a subjective case of the pronoun is required.

Follow the same procedure when considering pronouns that function as sentence objects.

The teacher yells at ~~we~~ us banjo players during every practice.

You wouldn't say *The teacher yells at we*. The word *us* functions here as an indirect object, so the objective case is most appropriate.

COMPARISONS USING *THAN* OR *AS*

When making comparisons using *than* or *as*, writers frequently leave out words because these words are clearly understood by readers.

Last year Bill Gates made more money *than* I ~~made~~.

The case of the pronoun is determined by its function in the implied part of the sentence, which has been omitted. To determine the correct pronoun case in a sentence that uses *than* or *as* to make a comparison, supply the implied or missing part of the sentence. Then, decide if the pronoun case is correct.

The groom is a full metre taller than ~~her~~ she.

When the omitted words are supplied, the sentence reads: *The groom is a full metre taller than she [is]*. *She* is the subject of the verb *is*; therefore, the subjective case of the pronoun is required.

My late grandmother left my cousin as many family heirlooms as ~~I~~ me.

When the omitted words are supplied, the sentence reads: *My late grandmother left my cousin as many family heirlooms as [she left] me*. *Me* is the indirect object of *left*.

WITH INFINITIVES

The infinitive is the base (simple) form of a verb, usually following *to*, as in *to jump*. Both the subject and the object of an infinitive are in the objective case.

As the Subject of an Infinitive
The minister asked <u>her</u> [not *she*] to sing at the wedding.

As the Object of an Infinitive
Club members decided to elect <u>him</u>.

POSSESSIVE CASE WHEN MODIFYING A GERUND

A **gerund** is a form of a verb that ends in *-ing* and is used as a noun; for example, *Fencing is my favourite sport*. Use a pronoun in the possessive case (*my, our, your, her/his/its, their*) to modify a gerund or gerund phrases.

> his
> The physical trainer disapproved of ~~him~~ eating bacon before workouts.

Nouns as well as pronouns can modify gerunds; as with pronouns, you must use the possessive case of the noun. The possessive is formed by adding an apostrophe and -s to the end of the noun.

> <u>Wayne's</u> smoking is the cause of his bad breath.

> Wayne's
> The physical trainer disapproved of ~~Wayne~~ eating bacon before workouts.

WHO AND WHOM

Who and *whom* are pronouns. *Who* is the subjective case; it must be used only for subjects and subject complements. *Whom* is the objective case; it must be used only for objects.

Who and *whom* are used as interrogative pronouns to open questions. They are also used as relative pronouns, to introduce subordinate clauses.

AS INTERROGATIVE PRONOUNS OPENING QUESTIONS

To decide whether to use *who* or *whom*, you must first determine the pronoun's function within the question. Does the interrogative pronoun function as a subject or subject complement, or as an object? Determine whether the subjective or objective case is required by recasting the question as a statement—that is, giving a possible answer to the question. Temporarily substitute a subjective case pronoun, such as *he*, or an objective case pronoun, such as *him*.

> Who
> ~~Whom~~ commanded the coalition forces during the war in Afghanistan?

A possible answer would be *He commanded the coalition forces. Him commanded* would not work. He is the subject of the verb *commanded*. Therefore, the subjective case is required, and *who* is the correct interrogative pronoun.

> Whom
> ~~Who~~ did the human resources manager interview?

A possible answer to the question would be *The human resources manager interviewed her. Interviewed she* would not work. *Her* would be the direct object of the verb *did interview*.

Therefore, the objective case is required, and *whom* is the correct interrogative pronoun.

AS RELATIVE PRONOUNS INTRODUCING SUBORDINATE CLAUSES

Use *who* and *whoever* as relative pronouns for subjects and use *whom* and *whomever* for objects. When deciding which pronoun to use, you must determine whether the relative pronoun functions as a subject or object within the subordinate clause. A good technique to employ when making this decision is to mentally block off the subordinate clause you are considering.

> *whoever*
> The Nobel Prize for Literature is presented to [~~whomever~~ has made the most significant contribution to literature over the course of a writing career.]

When determining the correct relative pronoun, consider only the subordinate clause. Hence, the main clause (*The Nobel Prize for Literature is presented to*) is mentally set aside. The relative pronoun of the subordinate clause is the subject of the verb *has made*. The subjective pronoun case is required; thus, the relative pronoun *whoever* is the correct choice. Notice that the entire subordinate clause functions as the object of the preposition *to*.

> *whom*
> We don't know [~~who~~ the university president nominated to chair the committee.]

Mentally set aside *We don't know* to enable you to focus exclusively on the subordinate clause. The relative pronoun is the object of the verb *nominated*. Thus, the objective case is required, and the correct pronoun is *whom*.

Do not be misled by interrupting expressions such as *I know*, *they think*, or *she believes*, which often come after *who* or *whom* in a subordinate clause.

> *who*
> The car dealer intends to invite only the customers [~~whom~~ *he thinks* will want to attend.]

Mentally set aside *The car dealer intends to invite only the customers* and *he thinks*. The relative pronoun of the remaining subordinate clause is the subject of the verb *will want*. Therefore, the subjective case is required, and the correct relative pronoun is *who*.

Subject–Verb Agreement

Every sentence has a subject (stated or implied) and a verb. **Subject–verb agreement** refers to the relationship between the subject and the verb.

In the present tense, verbs must agree with subjects in two ways.

1. In **number**. Number means the subject can be singular (e.g., *I*) or plural (e.g., *we*).
2. In **person**. Person can be first person (*I*, *we*), second person (*you*) or third person (*she*, *he*, *it*, or *they*).

If the verb is a regular verb and the subject is in the third-person singular, use the *-s* (or *-es*) form of the verb.

<u>Amir</u> *works* for his godfather.

His <u>godfather</u> *stresses* the importance of being on time.

PRESENT-TENSE FORMS OF *WORK*		
	SINGULAR	PLURAL
First person	I *work*	we *work*
Second person	you *work*	you *work*
Third person	she/he/it *works*	they *work*

Notice how the following irregular verbs achieve subject–verb agreement.

PRESENT-TENSE FORMS OF *DO*	
I *do*	we *do*
you *do*	you *do*
she/he/it *does*	they *do*

PRESENT-TENSE FORMS OF *HAVE*	
I *have*	we *have*
you *have*	you *have*
she/he/it *has*	they *have*

The verb *to be* has different forms for the present and past tense.

PRESENT-TENSE FORMS OF *BE*	
I *am*	we *are*
you *are*	you *are*
she/he/it *is*	they *are*

PAST-TENSE FORMS OF *BE*	
I *was*	we *were*
you *were*	you *were*
she/he/it *was*	they *were*

Often, if you have been speaking or writing English for a long time or know it well, problems with subject–verb agreement will be obvious to your ear or eye. For example, the sentence *James look good in his new tuxedo* immediately sounds or looks incorrect. It is obvious that the subject and verb do not agree. The sentence should be *James looks good in his new tuxedo.*

However, some subject–verb agreement problems are more difficult to spot. A number of English sentence constructions make the subject difficult to identify—often the subject is located far from the verb—and, as a result, it is easy to make verb-agreement mistakes. Information in the following section will help you to avoid the most common subject–verb agreement problems.

WORDS BETWEEN SUBJECT AND VERB

Occasionally the modifying words between the sentence subject and verb include a noun, which might be mistaken for the subject. As a result, some writers use a verb that does not agree with the actual subject.

When evaluating any sentence for subject–verb agreement, in your mind, delete any modifying elements, such as prepositional phrases, so that only the sentence subject and verb remain. Then, assess whether or not the subject and verb agree. You might consider drawing an arrow to connect the subject with the verb, as has been done in the example below.

The <u>first ten minutes</u> of a blind date *are* the most frightening.

practise
The <u>women</u> in my residence ~~practises~~ kung fu for hours every day.

The subject of the sentence above is *women*, not *residence*. The sentence verb is *practise*. Since the subject is in the third person plural, the correct verb form is *practise*, not *practises*.

The <u>objective</u> in both cases ~~are~~ *is* to give the students hands-on experience dealing with real-life situations.

The subject of the sentence is *objective*, not *cases*. The sentence verb is a form of the verb *to be*. The subject, *objective*, is in the third-person singular. To be correct, the verb form should be *is*, not *are*.

Phrases beginning *along with*, *as well as*, *in addition to*, and *together with* do not change the number of the subject because they are not really part of the subject. They are prepositional phrases used to modify the subject only.

The <u>prime minister,</u> along with the cabinet, was photographed in the glamour shot.

The *prime minister* is the main subject of the sentence. If the writer had wanted to emphasize both the prime minister and the cabinet, he or she might have structured the sentence as follows: *The prime minister and the cabinet were photographed in the glamour shot.*

SUBJECTS WITH *AND*

A compound subject contains two or more independent subjects joined by *and*. The compound subject requires a plural verb.

<u>Tina and Mauri</u> were inseparable.

The American bulldog's unforgettable <u>face and</u> amazing athletic <u>ability</u> ~~has~~ *have* helped to make Harley a star of advertising media.

However, when the parts of the subject refer to a single person or idea, they require a singular verb.

<u>Rice and tomato</u> *is* a San Francisco treat.

<u>Spaghetti and clam sauce</u> *has* been a favourite in our house for years.

The pronoun *each* is singular and requires a singular verb, even if the subjects it precedes are joined by *and*.

Each <u>woman</u> and <u>man</u> *is* allowed one vote.

SUBJECTS WITH *OR* OR *NOR*

When a compound subject is joined by *or* or *nor*, make the verb agree with the part of the subject nearer to the verb.

Neither the tour guide <u>nor his passengers</u> *know* if the CN Tower is the world's tallest building.

Either the Beatles <u>or Elvis Presley</u> *has* had the most gold albums.

are
If my aunt or my <u>cousins</u> ~~is~~ available, they will come to the quilting bee.

is
Neither the cabinet members nor the <u>prime minister</u> ~~are~~ going to wave to the crowd.

INDEFINITE PRONOUNS

An **indefinite pronoun** refers to an unspecified person or thing. The following are indefinite pronouns:

all, anybody, anyone, anything, each, either, everybody, everyone, everything, neither, no one, nobody, none, nothing, one, some, somebody, someone, something

Even though many indefinite pronouns seem to refer to more than one person or thing, most require a singular verb. Note especially that *each, either,* and words ending in *-body* and *-one* are singular.

<u>Everybody</u> from our class *was* at the nudist colony.

smells
<u>Something</u> in the garage ~~smell~~ fishy.

pays
<u>Everyone</u> in our house ~~pay~~ bills on time.

NEITHER AND *NONE*
When used alone, the indefinite pronouns *neither* and *none* require singular verbs.

<u>Neither</u> *is* correct.

Of the guests who were sent RSVP invitations, <u>none</u> *has* deigned to respond.

When prepositional phrases with plurals follow the indefinite pronouns *neither* and *none*, in some cases a plural or singular verb may be used. However, it is best to treat *neither* and *none* consistently as singular.

Neither of those flattering adjectives *applies* to my parents.

None of these programs *offers* bonus air miles.

INDEFINITE PRONOUNS THAT CAN BE SINGULAR OR PLURAL

A few indefinite pronouns, such as *all*, *any*, *more*, *most*, *none*, and *some*, can be singular or plural, depending on the noun or pronoun to which they refer.

Singular: All of the money *is* in a Swiss bank account.

Plural: All of his accounts *are* frozen because of the terrorist connection.

In the first example, *money* is a singular noun, so a singular verb is required. In the second example, *accounts* is a plural noun, so a plural verb is required.

COLLECTIVE NOUNS

A collective noun names a class or a group of people or things. Some examples of collective nouns include *band*, *committee*, *family*, *group*, *jury*, and *team*.

Use a singular verb with the collective noun when you want to communicate that the group is acting as a unit.

The band *agrees* that it *needs* a new drummer.

has
The first-year law class ~~have~~ a test on Monday.

The class and *the band* are considered single units, and individual action is not important to the sentence meaning. Therefore, a singular verb is required.

Use a plural verb when you want to communicate that members of the group are acting independently.

The original band *have* gone on to pursue solo careers and spend time in rehabilitation centres.

have
The first-year law class ~~has~~ their fingerprints on file.

Each member of the class has his or her fingerprints on file.

Sometimes it is possible to better capture the idea of individual action by recasting the sentence with a plural noun.

The <u>original band members</u> *have* gone on to pursue solo careers and spend time in rehabilitation centres.

DECIDING WHETHER TO TREAT **NUMBER** *AS A SINGULAR OR PLURAL*

If the collective noun *number* is preceded by *the*, treat it as a singular noun.

<u>The number</u> of ways to cheat death *is* increasing.

If *number* is preceded by *a*, treat it as a plural.

<u>A number</u> of Scrabble players *have* gotten a triple word score.

UNITS OF MEASUREMENT

Use a singular verb when the unit of measurement is used collectively, that is, when the thing described by the noun cannot be counted.

<u>One-half</u> of the <u>fat</u> in those French fries *is* unsaturated.

Use a plural verb when the unit of measurement refers to individual persons or things that can be counted.

Only <u>one-half</u> of your <u>promises</u> *are* likely to be kept.

SUBJECT AFTER VERB

Most often the verb follows the subject in sentences. However, in certain cases, the verb may come before the subject, making it difficult to evaluate subject–verb agreement.

EXPLETIVE CONSTRUCTIONS

Expletive constructions include phrases such as *there is, there are,* it is, and it *was.* When these phrases appear at the beginning of a sentence, the verb often precedes the subject.

There *are* significant <u>differences</u> among the pop stars of the '60s.

INVERTING SENTENCE ORDER

To achieve sentence variety, you may from time to time wish to invert traditional subject–verb order. Ensure that when you do this, you check that the subject and the verb agree.

are

Nestled on the couch ~~is~~ <u>a beautiful black malamute and a spectacular red setter</u>.

The compound subject, *a beautiful black malamute and a spectacular red setter*, requires a plural verb.

SUBJECT COMPLEMENT

A *subject complement* is a noun or adjective that follows a linking verb and renames or describes the sentence subject, as in *Elvis Presley is a cult figure*. Because of its relationship to the subject, the complement can often be mistaken for the subject and result in subject–verb agreement errors.

is

The socialite's central <u>concern</u> ~~are~~ facial lines.

The subject of the sentence is *concern*, which is singular. If the subject is singular, the sentence requires a singular verb. The plural *lines* is the complement.

are

<u>The advice column and the comics</u> ~~is~~ all I read in the newspaper.

The subject of the sentence is *the advice column and the comics*. Since it is plural, it requires a plural verb.

WITH RELATIVE PRONOUNS

WHO, WHICH, AND THAT

A relative pronoun such as *who, which*, or *that* usually introduces an adjective clause that modifies the subject. The relative pronoun must agree with its antecedent. The antecedent is the noun or pronoun to which the relative pronoun refers. Thus, the verb in the adjective clause must agree with the antecedent.

The wealthy <u>industrialist</u> who *donates* money to the food bank *expects* a tax deduction.

The singular noun *industrialist* is the antecedent of *who*. The verb *donates* must then be singular.

CONSTRUCTIONS USING **ONE OF THE** *AND* **THE ONLY ONE OF THE**

Subject–verb agreement mistakes are often made with relative pronouns when the sentence contains *one of the* or *the only one of the*.

Generally, use a plural verb with constructions containing *one of the*.

> *cause*
> The stiletto heel is one of the styles of footwear that ~~causes~~ a
> lot of medical problems.

The antecedent of *that* is *styles*, not *heel* or *footwear*. Since the
antecedent is plural, to agree, the verb *cause* must also be
plural.

Generally, use a singular verb with constructions containing
the only one of the.

> *is*
> The roller coaster is *the only one of the* rides <u>that</u> ~~are~~ worth
> the price.

The antecedent of *that* is *one*, not *rides*. Since the antecedent is
singular, to agree, the verb must also be singular: *is*.

PLURAL FORM, SINGULAR MEANING

Some words ending in -ics or -s are singular in meaning, even
though they may seem plural in appearance. These words
include *athletics, economics, ethics, physics, politics, statistics,
mathematics, measles, mumps,* and *news.* Nouns such as these
generally require a singular verb.

> *was*
> <u>The news</u> ~~were~~ encouraging.

When nouns such as *mathematics, physics,* and *statistics* refer
to a particular item of knowledge, as opposed to the collective
body of knowledge, they are treated as plural.

> Environment Canada <u>statistics</u> *reveal* that the area experi-
> enced record amounts of smog.

TITLES AND WORDS AS WORDS

A work referred to by its title is treated as a singular entity,
even if the title includes a plural word.

> *deals*
> *Dog Days* ~~deal~~ with the hilarious consequences of Peter's dis-
> enchantment with his job.

> *refers*
> In this report, "<u>illegal aliens</u>" ~~refer~~ to people who enter the
> country without following prescribed immigration proce-
> dures.

Adverbs and Adjectives

Adjectives and adverbs are modifiers. Adjectives modify nouns and pronouns. Adverbs can modify

- verbs

  He left the examination *early*.

- adjectives

  Her cheeks were *slightly* red.

- other adverbs

  They ate dinner *very* late.

Many adverbs end in -ly (*quickly, oddly*); however, some do not (*often, very*). As well, a number of adjectives end in -ly (*lovely*).

Problems can occur when adjectives are incorrectly used as adverbs or vice versa. The best way to decide whether a modifier should be an adjective or an adverb is to determine its function in the sentence. If you are in doubt about whether a word is an adjective or an adverb, you might also consult a good Canadian dictionary.

ADVERBS

In modifying a verb, another adverb, or an adjective, an adverb answers questions such as why? when? where? how? The following are some common misuses of adjectives in situations where adverbs are required:

1. Using adjectives to modify verbs

    The choir ~~sang loud~~ and ~~clear~~ at the concert.
    ^{loudly}   ^{clearly}

2. Using the adjective *good* when the adverb *well* is required

    The minister of education indicated to the media that he

    wants students within the province to be able to <u>write</u> ~~good~~ ^{well}

    For more detail on the correct uses of *good* and *well*, see the usage glossary at the back of this guide.

3. Using adjectives to modify adjectives or adverbs

    The museum in Niagara Falls has a ~~real~~ <u>unusual</u> collection of artifacts. ^{really}

ADJECTIVES

Usually adjectives come before the nouns or pronouns they modify.

> She watched the *red* <u>dawn</u>.

However, adjectives can also function as subject complements that follow a linking verb. The subject complement renames or describes the sentence subject.

> <u>Silence</u> is *golden*.

Linking verbs communicate states of being as opposed to actions.

> The <u>milk</u> at the back of the refrigerator *tasted* ~~sourly.~~ *sour*

> <u>She</u> *seems* ~~happily.~~ *happy*

> When my headache returned, <u>I</u> <u>felt</u> ~~badly.~~ *bad*

In these examples, the verbs *taste, seem,* and *feel* communicate states of being that modify the subject, so adjectives are required.

Some verbs, such as *look, feel, smell,* and *taste,* may or may not be linking verbs. When the word after the verb modifies the subject, the verb is a linking verb, and this modifying word should be an adjective. However, when the word modifies the verb, it should be an adverb.

Modifying the Subject
The girl looked <u>curious</u>.

Curious modifies the subject, *girl.* Here, *looked* is a linking verb and the modifier is an adjective. The adjective *curious* describes the girl's state of being.

Modifying the Verb
The girl looked <u>curiously</u> at the man dressed in a bunny suit.

Here, *curiously* modifies the verb, *looked.* The adverb *curiously* describes how the act of looking was done.

COMPARATIVES AND SUPERLATIVES

1. the positive
2. the comparative
3. the superlative

Adjectives

POSITIVE	COMPARATIVE	SUPERLATIVE
One- and most two-syllable adjectives		
red	redder	reddest
crazy	crazier	craziest
Longer adjectives		
intoxicating	more intoxicating	most intoxicating
selfish	less selfish	least selfish
Irregular		
good	better	best
bad	worse	worst
No comparative or superlative form		
unique	—	—
pregnant	—	—

Adverbs

POSITIVE	COMPARATIVE	SUPERLATIVE
Ending in -ly		
selfishly	more selfishly	most selfishly
gracefully	less gracefully	least gracefully
Not ending in -ly		
fast	faster	fastest
Irregular		
well	better	best
badly	worse	worst
No comparative or superlative form		
really	—	—
solely	—	—

WHEN TO USE THE COMPARATIVE FORM AND WHEN TO USE THE SUPERLATIVE FORM

When comparing two entities, use the comparative form.

Which is the ~~least~~ lesser of the two evils?

The jaguar moves ~~fastest~~ faster than the lion.

When comparing three or more entities, use the superlative.

Of all the playwrights, I feel that William Shakespeare is the *greatest*.

most

She is the ~~more~~ selfish of the three sisters.

DO NOT USE DOUBLE COMPARATIVES OR SUPERLATIVES

Of the two playwrights, I feel that William Shakespeare is the ~~more~~ greater.

beautiful

The painting is probably one of the most ~~beautifulest~~ in the museum.

DO NOT USE COMPARATIVES OR SUPERLATIVES WITH ABSOLUTE CONCEPTS

Absolute concepts by their very nature do not come in degrees and cannot be compared. Some examples of absolute concepts are *favourite, unique, perfect, pregnant, impossible, infinite,* or *priceless.* If two diamonds are perfect, one cannot be more perfect than the other. Similarly, of three perfect diamonds, one cannot be most perfect.

Incorrect: The cat looks <u>more pregnant</u> than she did last week.

Correct: The cat's pregnancy is more obvious than it was last week.

That painting by Leonardo da Vinci is ~~very~~ unique.

unusual

The bizarre comedy was the most ~~unique~~ I have ever seen.

DOUBLE NEGATIVES

Two negatives are acceptable in a sentence only if they create a positive meaning.

She was <u>not</u> <u>unhappy</u> with her ten-game hitting streak.

A **double negative** is a non-standard English construction in which negative modifiers such as *no, not, neither, none, nothing,* and *never* are paired to cancel each other. Double negatives should be avoided in any formal writing.

The government ~~never~~ does <u>nothing</u> to solve the problems affecting the poor.

anything

Barry did not feel ~~nothing~~ during his hernia operation.

In standard English, the modifiers *barely*, *hardly*, and *scarcely* are considered negative modifiers. These words should not be paired with words such as *no*, *not*, or *never*.

They could ~~not~~ <u>barely</u> hear the tiny girl speak.

Problems with Modifiers

A modifier is a word, phrase, or clause that describes or limits another word, phrase, or clause within a sentence. Modifiers must be placed carefully and correctly or they will cloud—or, in some instances, destroy—sentence meaning. Generally, modifying words should be kept close to the words they modify.

LIMITING MODIFIERS SUCH AS *ONLY* AND *EVEN*

Place limiting words such as *just, even, only, almost, hardly, nearly*, and *merely* directly before the verb they modify.

She *nearly* <u>missed</u> the swim team's practice.

If a limiting word modifies another word in the sentence, place the modifier in front of that word.

Incorrect: In the first quarter, Steve Nash did not *even* score <u>one point</u>.

Correct: In the first quarter, Steve Nash did not score *even* <u>one point</u>.

In this example, *even* must modify *one point* instead of *score*, so the modifier should be placed in front of *one point*.

Incorrect: Louis Cyr *only* weighed <u>250 pounds</u>.

Correct: Louis Cyr weighed *only* <u>250 pounds</u>.

Here, *only* must modify *250 pounds* instead of *weighed*, so the modifier should be placed in front of *250 pounds*.

The modifier *not* is often misplaced, a situation that can create confusing or unintended meanings.

Unintended Meaning: All snake bites are *not* lethal.

Intended Meaning: *Not* all snake bites are lethal.

In the first version, one possible meaning is that no snake bite is lethal, which could be a dangerous assumption in certain parts of the world. The correction makes the meaning clear: one does not have to worry that all snake bites are lethal.

MISPLACED PHRASES AND CLAUSES

A **misplaced modifier** is a describing word, phrase, or clause that is incorrectly positioned within a sentence so that the modifier's meaning is illogical or unclear. The misplaced modifier relates to, or modifies, the wrong word or words in the sentence. When a modifier is misplaced, unusual misreadings can result.

- ✗ Jennifer sat waiting for her boyfriend <u>to park the car in a slinky red dress with a plunging neckline</u>.

- ✔ <u>In a slinky red dress with a plunging neckline, Jennifer sat waiting</u> for her boyfriend to park the car.

When the modifier is placed so far from what it modifies, the reader could easily conclude that it is Jennifer's boyfriend who is wearing the slinky dress.

- ✗ The counter clerk at the soda fountain brought the sundae to <u>the eager young boy covered in chocolate sauce</u>.

- ✔ The counter clerk at the soda fountain brought <u>the sundae covered in chocolate sauce</u> to the eager young boy.

The first sentence can be misinterpreted two ways: either the clerk or the boy was covered in chocolate sauce.

- ✗ A beautiful painting attracts <u>the viewer's eye on the wall of the National Gallery</u>.

- ✔ <u>A beautiful painting on the wall of the National Gallery</u> attracts the viewer's eye.

The painting, not the viewer's eye, is on the wall.

Sometimes modifier placement can lead to ambiguity so that two or more revisions are possible. The correction chosen will depend on the writer's intended meaning.

Ambiguous: The fellow <u>we interviewed at the station yesterday turned up in London</u>.

Clear: The fellow <u>we interviewed yesterday</u> at the station turned up in London.

Clear: The fellow <u>we interviewed at the station</u> turned up in London yesterday.

In the first sentence, it is unclear whether the fellow was interviewed yesterday or turned up in London yesterday.

AWKWARDLY PLACED MODIFIERS

Sentences should generally flow in a pattern from subject to verb to object. Keep the subject as close to the main verb as possible and, where possible, don't separate the subject from the main verb of the sentence with a modifying adverb clause.

> *Awkward:* The dog, <u>after chasing the mail carrier</u>, wagged its tail and pranced triumphantly to the front porch.

> *Clear:* <u>After chasing the mail carrier</u>, the dog wagged its tail and pranced triumphantly to the front porch.

There is no reason to separate the subject *dog* from the verb *wagged* with a fairly long modifying clause.

As well, keep auxiliary verbs near to the main verbs.

> *Awkward:* <u>I have</u> as long as I can remember had a scar on my elbow.

> *Clear:* I <u>have had</u> a scar on my elbow as long as I can remember.

The complete verb is *have had*, so the main and auxiliary verb should be placed together.

SPLIT INFINITIVES

An infinitive consists of *to* and the verb, as in *to love*, *to leave*, and *to forget*. In a *split infinitive*, a modifier is placed between *to* and the verb. Frequently, including a split infinitive in a sentence will make the sentence awkward, and the sentence will need to be revised. One famous example of a split infinitive is in the opening to *Star Trek*, "To boldly go where no man has gone before"; it is parodied by Douglas Adams in *The Hitchhiker's Guide to the Galaxy*: "Men boldly split infinitives that no man had split before." Split infinitives are not considered grammatical errors in modern writing and are often very effective usage, but they are easy to spot, so use them at your peril.

> *Awkward:* Financial analysts expected the stock prices <u>to</u>, after a period of sharp decline, dramatically rise.

> *Clear:* Financial analysts expected the stock prices <u>to rise</u> dramatically after a period of share decline.

Here the phrasing is awkward because of a long intervening phrase that splits the infinitive. A similar case is illustrated below:

> *Awkward:* Try <u>to</u>, if you can get it, <u>see</u> her latest DVD.

> *Clear:* Try to see her latest DVD, if you can get it.

However, in some instances, split infinitives are preferable to alternative wordings. It might be argued that the following split infinitive is essential because of a slight nuance in meaning:

The audience failed <u>to</u> completely <u>understand</u> the argument.

This may mean that that the audience's understanding was incomplete, but not that their failure was complete, as it would in this example where the infinitive is not split:

The audience failed <u>completely</u> *to understand* the argument.

Generally, avoid split infinitives in formal writing. They are often pointed out as errors, even though they are quite common in informal writing and are not errors.

DANGLING MODIFIERS

A **dangling modifier** is a word, phrase, or clause that does not relate to any word within the sentence and, as a result, confuses the reader. Dangling modifiers usually appear at the start of the sentence, and the person who performs the action is not mentioned. A dangling modifier can be one of the following:

- a participial phrase

  <u>Believed to be dangerous</u>, an old lady was accosted on the street.

- a gerund phrase

  <u>After eating dinner</u>, the turkey was left sitting on the table.

- an infinitive phrase

  To win first place on a reality-TV show, a strong stomach is needed.

To repair dangling modifier problems, use one of the following revision strategies:

PROVIDE THE SUBJECT OF THE SENTENCE IMMEDIATELY AFTER THE DANGLING PHRASE

- ✗ <u>Believed to be dangerous</u>, an old lady was accosted on the street.

- ✔ <u>Believed to be dangerous, an escaped convict</u> accosted an old lady on the street.

A new subject must be added.

- ✗ <u>After eating dinner</u>, the turkey was left sitting on the table.

- ✔ <u>After eating dinner, we</u> left the turkey sitting on the table.

The implied subject of the gerund phrase is explicitly stated.

> ✗ To win first place on a reality-TV show, a strong stomach is needed.

> ✔ To win first place on a reality-TV show, a contestant needs a strong stomach.

The implied subject of the infinitive phrase is explicitly stated.

Also watch out for elliptical phrases. The subject of the participle must be explicitly stated in order to avoid dangling modifiers.

> ✗ Keep stirring the meat until browned.

As it stands, this sentence implies that the person stirring the meat is being browned, not the meat.

> ✔ Keep stirring the meat <u>until it is browned</u>.

To assess whether or not a sentence you have written has a dangling modifier, apply the following questioning strategy:

1. Does the word group have a verb?
   - ❏ YES. Consider the next question.
   - ❏ NO. *The word group is a fragment and must be revised to include a verb.*

2. Does the participial phrase suggest an action without indicating who is performing the action?
   - ❏ NO. You do not have a dangling modifier problem.
   - ❏ YES. Consider the next question.

3. Does the subject of the independent clause indicate who performs the action?
   - ❏ YES. You do not have a dangling modifier problem.
   - ❏ NO. *Apply one of the three strategies listed above to address the dangling modifier problem.*

Shifts

A **shift** is a sudden and unnecessary change in point of view, verb tense, mood, or voice, or a change from indirect to direct questions or quotations. Shifts can occur within and between sentences. They often blur meaning and confuse readers.

POINT OF VIEW

In writing, **point of view** is the perspective from which the work is written. Often this is indicated by the pronouns the writer uses.

1. First person: *I, we*
2. Second person: *you*
3. Third person: *he/she/it/one* or *they*

You have probably noticed the following in the course of your own writing and reading:

- The first-person point of view often appears in more informal types of writing, such as journals, diaries, and personal letters.
- The second-person point of view is often found in directions or instructional types of writing, such as this handbook.
- The third-person point of view emphasizes the subject. It is used in informative writing, including the writing you do in many academic and professional contexts.

Shifts in point of view occur when a writer begins his or her piece of writing in one point of view, then shifts carelessly back and forth to other points of view. To prevent needless shifts, think about the most appropriate point of view for your writing situation, establish the point of view in your writing, and keep to that point of view.

Shifts in Point of View
Some hikers have their dogs carry the food pack on longer

their
trips. As ~~our~~ journey progresses and stops are periodically made for meals, the dog's pack becomes lighter.

The writer started the passage in the third person, then shifted to the first person with *our*.

Your fax machine supports both tone and pulse dialling. The
you do
default setting is TONE, so ~~one does~~ not need to change the
you use
setting if ~~he or she uses~~ that kind of line. If you are using a pulse dial line, change the setting to PULSE by following these steps.

In these instructions, the writer began in the second person, then shifted to the third person before returning to the second person.

A common problem among student writers is shifting from the third-person singular to the third-person plural or vice versa.

Shift from Singular to Plural
they prefer
Since malamutes have very heavy fur coats, ~~it prefers to~~ sleep outside even in extremely cold temperatures.

The writer shifted from third-person plural (*malamutes*) to third-person singular (*it*).

VERB TENSE

The verb tense tells the reader when the action in the piece of writing is taking place. Shifting from one verb tense to another without a sound reason confuses the reader.

Tense Shift
He is so vain that he always sits at a restaurant table facing
                             thinks
the sunlight, since he ~~thought~~ the rays might add to his precious tan.

The sentence begins in the present tense (*sits*) then shifts to the past tense (*thought*).

The convention in essays about literature is to describe fictional events consistently in the present tense. Sometimes, of course, shifts in tense are necessary if you are discussing literature in its historical context.

D.H. Lawrence's use of profane language was a departure from the conventions of the novel in the early twentieth century.

Shift from Literary Present
As an egocentric, Gabriel has "restless eyes" early in "The Dead." However, when he displays empathy near the end of
                   possesses
the story, he ~~possessed~~ "curious eyes."

The writer begins using the literary present tense convention, then erroneously shifts into the past tense with *possessed*.

VERB MOOD AND VOICE

MOOD
Shifts can also occur in the mood of verbs. The mood of the verb indicates the manner of action. There are three moods in English.

1. The indicative mood is used to state facts or opinions, or to ask questions.

   He wrote a short story.

   Did he win a prize for the story?

2. The imperative mood is used to give a command or advice, or make a request.

Don't do that!

Rewind the videotape before returning it.

3. The subjunctive mood is used to express doubt, wishes, or possibility.

If I were lucky, I might have won the lottery.

The subjunctive mood also expresses conditions contrary to fact.

If wishes were horses, beggars would ride.

Mood Shift
Include more foreground by focusing in front of your main subject while keeping the subject within the depth of field. ~~The reverse is also true.~~ To include more background, do the reverse.

The writer's purpose is to give advice on photography. He or she appropriately begins in the imperative mood, but erroneously shifts into the indicative mood.

VOICE
Voice refers to whether a verb is active or passive. A verb is active when the subject is the doer of the action. A verb is passive when the subject of the verb receives the action. If the writer suddenly shifts between voices, it can be jarring and confusing to the reader.

Shift in Voice
I could immediately comprehend the devastation of the avalanche as soon as I reached the peak overlooking the valley ~~was reached~~.

The subordinate clause is in the passive voice, while the main clause is in the active voice.

DIRECT AND INDIRECT QUESTIONS OR QUOTATIONS

DIRECT AND INDIRECT QUOTATIONS
In a direct quotation, the writer repeats a speaker's words exactly, placing those words within quotation marks. In an indirect quotation, the writer summarizes or paraphrases what the speaker has said.

Direct: U.S. General William C. Westmoreland said, "We'll blow them back into the Stone Age."

Indirect: U.S. General William C. Westmoreland said his forces would bomb the enemy so relentlessly that they would be blown back into the Stone Age.

Shift from Indirect to Direct

The dog trainer told me to keep Pepé by my side and ~~don't~~ *not* give the dog more than a foot of slack on his lead.

The writer shifts from indirect quotation to direct quotation with *don't give the dog more than a foot of slack on his lead.* The revision makes the quotation consistently indirect. An alternative revision would be *The dog trainer said, "Keep Pepé by your side and don't give the dog more than a foot of slack on his lead."* In this version, the quotation is consistently direct.

DIRECT AND INDIRECT QUESTIONS

A direct question stands alone as a question. It is not introduced or included in any statement.

Which road do you take to get to Lions Head?

An indirect question reports that a question was asked, but does not actually ask the question.

I asked which road to take to get to Lions Head.

Shifting from indirect to direct questions can make writing awkward and confusing.

Shift from Indirect to Direct

I'm asking ~~you if you'd like~~ *whether you'd like* to hike the Bruce Trail, and if so, would you like to start at Tobermory or St. Catharines.

The revision presents both questions indirectly. An alternate revision would be to pose both questions directly: *Would you like to hike the Bruce Trail, and if so, would you like to start at Tobermory or St. Catharines?*

Mixed Constructions

A sentence with a **mixed construction** incorrectly changes from one grammatical construction to another incompatible one, thereby confusing the sentence's meaning.

MIXED GRAMMAR

When you draft a sentence, your options for structuring that sentence are limited by the grammatical patterns of English. You must consistently follow the pattern you choose within the sentence. You cannot start the sentence using one grammatical pattern and then abruptly change to another. *Don't switch horses* [grammatical structures] *in the middle of a stream* [sentence] is an idiom that can help you remember this key grammatical guideline.

Mixed: By multiplying the number of specialty stations available to viewers via digital television increases the chance that cultural communities within Canada's diverse cultural mosaic will be better served.

Revised: <u>Multiplying</u> the number of specialty stations available to viewers via digital television <u>increases</u> the chance that cultural communities within Canada's diverse cultural mosaic will be better served.

OR

Revised: <u>By multiplying</u> the number of specialty stations available to viewers via digital television, <u>satellite and cable companies increase</u> the chance that cultural communities within Canada's diverse cultural mosaic will be better served.

The mixed construction, which begins with *by*, cannot serve as the subject of the sentence. In the first revision, *by* is dropped, so the opening is no longer a participial phrase but is now a gerund and hence the subject. In the second revision, the participial phrase is retained, but a subject is added so that the phrase is not a dangling modifier.

Another mixed construction is incorrectly combined clauses.

~~Although satellite~~ Satellite dishes have become popular in many northern Canadian communities, but many viewers still prefer local stations.

Here the clause beginning *although* is a subordinate clause. Hence, it cannot be linked to an independent clause with the coordinating conjunction *but*.

From time to time, when revising your own work, you may encounter a sentence that can't be fixed grammatically. In instances such as this, it is often wise to rethink what you want to say, and then completely recast the sentence so it is clear, straightforward, and logical.

Mixed: In communicative language teaching, students' errors are corrected only when they interfere with comprehension rather than by the direct method in which students' errors are corrected immediately to avoid habit formation.

Revised: In communicative language teaching, students' errors are corrected only when they interfere with comprehension; <u>in the direct method, students' errors are corrected immediately</u> to avoid habit formation.

Often, trying to pack too much information into a sentence causes confusion.

ILLOGICAL CONNECTIONS

A number of sentence faults can occur when elements of the sentence do not logically fit together. **Faulty predication** is one example of such a problem. In faulty predication, the subject and predicate do not make sense together. To remedy this problem, either the subject or the predicate must be revised.

> *Originally,*
> ~~The original function of~~ the Internet was created to exchange academic and military information.

The function was not created to exchange academic and military information. In this instance, the subject is refined so that it connects more logically with the predicate.

> The decisions on who would make Canada's 2002 Olympic
> *were made*
> hockey team ~~was chosen~~ by a management committee headed by Wayne Gretzky.

The decisions didn't do the choosing. The management committee headed by Wayne Gretzky made the decisions.

An appositive is a noun or noun phrase that renames or explains a noun or noun phrase immediately before it; for example

> November, <u>the month of my birth</u>, . . .

The appositive must logically relate to the noun or noun phrase that precedes it; otherwise **faulty apposition** occurs.

> *speculation*
> Stock ~~speculators~~, <u>a very risky business</u>, demands nerves of steel and a healthy bank account.

Stock speculation, not stock speculators, is a very risky business.

AVOIDING *IS WHEN, IS WHERE, REASON . . . IS BECAUSE*

In formal writing, avoid the following constructions:

1. *Is when* or is *where*

In computer dating,

~~Computer dating is when~~ the computer is used to match potential romantic partners according to their compatibility, interests, and desirability.

Computer dating is not a time but a service.

2. *The reason . . . is because*

   ~~The reason~~ I watch horror movies ~~is~~ because I need a release from the tensions of life.

   Notice that the revised sentence is much tighter. The writer might also have avoided the awkward *reason . . . is because* construction by replacing *because* with *that*.

   These constructions are not grammatical and often add unnecessary words to a sentence. If you find such constructions in your drafts, revise the sentences that contain them.

Parallelism

Parallelism in writing means that equal grammatical structures are used to express equal ideas. Errors in parallelism, known as **faulty parallelism**, occur when *unequal* structures are used to express equal ideas. Words, phrases, and clauses should all be parallel when they express a similar idea and perform a similar function in a sentence. When using parallelism for effect, balance single words with single words, phrases with phrases, and clauses with clauses.

The following three quotations from Winston Churchill all demonstrate parallel, balanced elements:

Words: I have nothing to offer but blood, toil, tears, and sweat.

Phrases: Victory at all costs, victory in spite of all terror, victory however long and hard the road may be; for without victory there is no survival.

Clauses: You do your worst, and we will do our best.

WITH ITEMS IN A SERIES

When the reader encounters items in a series, he or she expects that parallel grammatical pattern to continue within the sentence. However, when one or more items do not follow the parallel grammatical pattern, the sentence seems jarring and awkward to the reader.

   ✗ Anatole liked the lawn, the hedge, and to garden.

   ✔ Anatole liked <u>the lawn, the hedge, and the garden.</u>

All items in the corrected version are nouns.

> ✗ Ace may not be the cutest or the largest dog in existence, but he's also very smart.

> ✔ Ace may not be the <u>cutest</u> or the <u>largest</u> dog in existence, but he may be one of the <u>smartest</u>.

Items in the corrected sentence are all comparative adjectives with the -*est* (or superlative) ending.

> ✗ Being outdoors, feeling the winds off the ocean, and to smell the Douglas fir are what I like about hiking British Columbia's West Coast Trail.

> ✔ <u>Being</u> outdoors, <u>feeling</u> the winds off the ocean, and <u>smelling</u> the Douglas fir are what I like about hiking British Columbia's West Coast Trail.

To smell must be in the -*ing* participial form to be consistent with *being* and *feeling*.

WITH PAIRED ITEMS

Parallel ideas are often connected in one of three ways:

1. with a coordinating conjunction, such as *or, and,* or *but*
2. with a pair of correlative conjunctions, such as *not only . . . but also* or *either . . . or*
3. with comparative constructions using *than* or *as*

Whenever you relate ideas using one of these methods, always emphasize the connection between or among ideas by expressing them in parallel grammatical form.

USING PARALLEL FORMS WITH COORDINATING CONJUNCTIONS

Coordinating conjunctions (*and, but, for, nor, or, so,* and *yet*) are words that connect ideas of equal importance. Avoid faulty parallelism by ensuring that all elements joined by coordinating conjunctions are parallel in grammatical form.

> ✗ Alfred, you may go by train, boat, car, bus, or a jet will take you there.

> ✔ Alfred, you may go by <u>train, boat, car, bus, or jet.</u>

In the original sentence, all elements in the series before the conjunction are nouns, but a clause is used for the last item, which is therefore not parallel.

> ✗ Our debating team read Jordan's ideas, were discussing her arguments, and have decided they are not relevant to our debate position.

Parallelism

✔ Our debating team <u>read</u> Jordan's ideas, <u>discussed</u> her arguments, and <u>decided</u> they are not relevant to our debate position.

The verb tenses *were discussing* and *have decided* are not consistent with the simple past tense *read*.

USING PARALLEL FORMS WITH CORRELATIVE CONJUNCTIONS
Correlative conjunctions are pairs of words that join equal grammatical structures. Examples include *not only . . . but also*, *either . . . or*, and *both . . . and*. Avoid faulty parallelism by ensuring that each element linked by correlative conjunctions is parallel in its grammatical form.

✗ When the staff met the sales target, the manager not only ordered new chairs, but also new desks, potted plants, and a microwave for the lunchroom.

✔ When the staff met the sales target, the manager ordered <u>not only</u> new chairs, <u>but also</u> new desks, potted plants, and a microwave for the lunchroom.

OR

✔ When the staff met the sales target, the manager <u>not only</u> ordered new chairs, <u>but also</u> provided new desks, potted plants, and a microwave for the lunchroom.

In the first revision, a noun follows *not only*, so a noun must follow *but also*. In the second, a verb follows *not only*; similarly, a verb must follow *but also*.

✗ Viewers either criticized the television station for its inflammatory views, or it was criticized for its political stance.

✔ Viewers <u>either</u> criticized the television station for its inflammatory views <u>or</u> criticized it for its political stance.

OR

✔ Viewers criticized the television station <u>either</u> for its inflammatory views <u>or</u> for its political stance.

The verb used with *either* must match the verb used with *or*, but in the original sentence, one is in the active voice, and the other is in the passive voice. The first revision corrects this problem; however, the second revision is more economical, and the connection between related ideas is even clearer.

COMPARISONS LINKED WITH *THAN* OR *AS*

Often you will use *than* or *as* to make comparisons. To avoid faulty parallelism, make sure the elements being compared are expressed using parallel grammatical structure.

> ✗ Having great wealth is not as satisfying as the completion of charitable works.

> ✔ <u>Having</u> great wealth is not as satisfying as <u>completing</u> charitable works.

Use the matching *-ing* form on both sides of the comparison.

> ✗ It is better to give than do the receiving.

> ✔ It is better <u>to give</u> than <u>to receive</u>.

Use the matching form—in this case, the infinitive form of the verb (with *to*)—on both sides of the comparison.

Note: With many of the corrections shown above, there are equally acceptable alternatives. In some instances, faulty parallelism corrections that occur to you may be improvements over what appears in the handbook.

" Style is a simple way of
saying complicated things. **"**

—JEAN COCTEAU

STYLE

Wordiness

Effective writing is concise, clear, and direct. Concise writing does not necessarily mean fewer words or shorter sentences. It means words that function clearly and sentences that express their point without empty words. A longer sentence may be considered extremely succinct if it is required to express a sophisticated idea. As well, many shorter sentences can be even more economically written. When revising, review each sentence you write with an eye to eliminating any phrase or word that is not absolutely necessary to your intended meaning.

REDUNDANCIES

Redundancy is the use of unnecessary words in a sentence. Often the same idea is expressed twice or more.

It is 6:30 a.m. in the morning.

Other common redundancies include final completion, important essentials, close proximity, consensus of opinion, and actual fact.

~~The reason~~ Nebuchadnezzar stopped his conquest ~~was~~ because he heard of his father's death and his own succession to the throne.

The board members did not want to repeat the debate ~~again~~, so they had a frank ~~and honest~~ discussion during which they identified some basic ~~essential~~ ideas.

When people are in ~~situations of~~ conflict at a meeting, they should circle ~~around~~ the speaker and ~~try to~~ attempt to ~~form a~~ *achieve* consensus ~~of opinion~~.

The bridge ~~that people cross to get~~ to Burlington is ~~sort of~~ rectangular ~~in shape~~, and it is made of strong materials such as reinforced steel, and concrete~~, etc~~.

UNNECESSARY REPETITION OF WORDS

Sometimes you may wish to repeat words or phrases to create an effect or for emphasis, as in parallel constructions. However, when words are repeated for no apparent reason, they make writing seem sloppy and awkward. As you revise, eliminate unnecessary repeated words.

The quarterback passed the football, but the lineman raised

his meaty, ~~heavy~~ hand and batted ~~the football~~ *it* away.

The houses ~~where the people live~~ are not far from ~~the city of~~ Moncton.

EMPTY OR INFLATED PHRASES

Occasionally, to make your writing sound more important, you may be tempted to include certain phrases you've heard others use. When you examine your sentences carefully, you'll find these padded phrases only increase your word count and contain little or no meaning. Effective writers state what they mean as simply and directly as possible. As you revise your work, trim sentences of any wordy, empty, or inflated phrases. These can often be spotted when you edit for conciseness. You don't need words like *I think* or *I feel* or *in my opinion*, for example, because your ownership as an author is established without them. Expressions like "in today's society" are also meaningless and should be avoided.

Because *currently*

~~By virtue of the fact that at the current time~~ we do not have sufficient funding, the skateboard park will not be built.

You can use concise words or phrases without affecting your meaning.

ELIMINATING WORDY OR INFLATED PHRASES	
WORDY/INFLATED	CONCISE
along the lines of	like
as a matter of fact	in fact
at all times	always
at the present time	now, currently, presently
at this point in time	now, currently, presently
because of the fact	because

WORDY/INFLATED	CONCISE
by means of	by
by virtue of the fact that	because
due to the fact that	because
for the purpose of	for
for the simple reason that	because
have a tendency to	tend
have the ability to	be able to
in the nature of	like
in order to	to
in spite of the fact that	although, even though
in the event that	if
in the final analysis	finally
in the neighbourhood of	about
in the world of today	today
it is necessary that	must
on the occasion of	when
prior to	before
until such a time as	until
with regard to	about

SIMPLIFYING STRUCTURE

The following word-trimming strategies will help you make your sentences simple, clear, and direct.

STRENGTHEN THE VERB

Often nouns derived from verbs can be turned back into verbs to make the sentence more direct and active.

During the strike, the ~~accumulation of~~ garbage ~~carried on~~ accumulated for fifteen days.

The noun phrase *accumulation of garbage* has been turned into the subject and verb *garbage accumulated*.

AVOID COLOURLESS VERBS

The verbs forms *is/are*, *was/were*, and *has/have/had* are weak and often create wordy sentence constructions.

> *recommends*
>
> The budget proposal before the legislature ~~is to do with~~ tax cuts and massive reductions in public-sector spending.

The weak verb *is* has been replaced with the more dynamic verb *recommends*.

REVISE EXPLETIVE CONSTRUCTIONS

An expletive construction uses *there* or *it* and a form of the verb *to be* in front of the sentence subject. Often these constructions create excess words. You might remove the expletive and revise the sentence to make it more concise and direct.

> A
>
> ~~There is a~~ picture of Pierre Trudeau playing baseball ~~that~~ shows the energy he brought to the prime minister's office.

> Most importantly,
>
> ~~It is important that~~ you should remain calm if your kayak capsizes in rough water.

WHERE POSSIBLE, USE THE ACTIVE VOICE

The active voice is generally more concise and direct than the passive voice. Use the active voice when you want to be direct and to focus on the action of a sentence.

> *Passive:* The research was conducted by senior students who plan to enter graduate school.

> *Active:* Senior students who plan to enter graduate school conducted the research.

Note: A grammar checker can easily find instances of the passive voice, but it is up to you to decide whether or not to make the suggested changes, based on your knowledge and the context of the document you are working on.

REDUCING CLAUSES AND PHRASES

In many instances, modifying clauses and phrases can be tightened. Where possible, reduce clauses to phrases and phrases to single words.

> As basketball fans, we journeyed to Almonte, Ontario, ~~which is~~ the birthplace of Canadian John Naismith.

> The powerful
>
> ~~Loaded with power, the~~ car was considered unbeatable.

Diction and Audience

The effectiveness of your writing will in large measure depend on the appropriateness of the language you decide to use for your audience. Choose the wording that best suits the context and the audience of your writing. Consider these elements as you choose your words:

- subject
- audience (their needs, expectations, and feelings)
- purpose
- voice (as reflected in your unique writing style)

The following section provides guidance and information that will help you to select appropriate language for your writing assignments.

JARGON

Jargon is the specialized language of a particular group or occupation. In some instances you may need to use jargon; for example, if your audience is the particular group or occupation that uses the jargon, or you can reasonably assume your audience will understand this specialized language. Generally, though, avoid jargon and use plain English instead.

Jargon: Positive input into the infrastructure impacts systematically on the functional base of the organization in that it stimulates meaningful objectives from a strategic standpoint.

Revised: Positive feedback to the organization helps it formulate concrete, strategic objectives.

Notice that the jargon made the meaning of the original sentence virtually incomprehensible; the writer needed to rethink his or her ideas completely, and then recast the sentence.

In addition to very specialized language, jargon often includes language that is intended to impress readers rather than to communicate information and ideas effectively. Jargon-filled language is often found in business, government, education, and military documents.

Sentences containing jargon are difficult to read and extremely unclear.

Jargon: The Director of Instruction implemented the optimal plan to ameliorate poor test scores among reading-at-risk students.

Clear: The Director of Instruction carried out the best plan to improve poor test scores among students having trouble reading.

Jargon: We will endeavour to facilitate a viable trash recovery initiative for all residences in the neighbourhood.

Clear: We will try to create a workable garbage pickup plan for all neighbourhood homes.

If you encounter inflated words or phrases in your writing draft, consider alternative words that are simple, clear, and precise in meaning.

ELIMINATING JARGON	
WORDS DESIGNED TO IMPRESS	**SIMPLE ALTERNATIVE(S)**
ameliorate	fix, improve
commence	begin, start
components	parts
endeavour	attempt, try
exit	go, leave
facilitate	help
factor	cause, consideration
finalize	complete, finish
impact on	effect
implement	carry out
indicator	sign
initiate	start, begin
optimal	best
parameters	boundaries, limits
prior to	before
prioritize	order, rank
utilize	use
viable	workable

PRETENTIOUS LANGUAGE, EUPHEMISMS

AVOID PRETENTIOUS LANGUAGE

When writing for academic audiences and purposes, it is tempting to opt for elevated language. However, using uncommon or unnecessarily long words can highlight rather than obscure deficiencies in content—and make the writing seem pretentious. Academic writing does not require that you use longer, difficult words for their own sake. State your ideas in words that you and your audience understand.

> *Pretentious:* It is *de rigueur* to expound on reification in Timothy Findley's fictional tome *The Wars.*

> *Plain Language:* It is necessary to discuss the treatment of people as objects in Timothy Findley's novel *The Wars.*

AVOID EUPHEMISMS

A **euphemism** is a word or expression intended to lessen the impact of harsh or unacceptable words or phrases. An example of a euphemism in a military context is *collateral damage*, a term sometimes used to describe civilian casualties. In a few writing situations, using euphemisms is acceptable. For instance, when expressing condolences to a friend you might use the euphemism *passed away* as a substitute for *died.* Generally, however, avoid euphemisms; they are highly indirect and blur meaning.

AVOIDING EUPHEMISMS

EUPHEMISM	PLAIN ENGLISH
chemical dependency	drug addiction
correctional facility	jail
declared redundant	fired, laid off
developing nations	poor countries
downsizing	laying off or firing employees
economically deprived	poor
incendiary device	bomb
laid to rest	buried
leather-like	vinyl

EUPHEMISM	PLAIN ENGLISH
military solution	war
misleading phrase	lie
pre-owned automobile	used car
starter home	small house
strategic withdrawal	defeat or retreat

SLANG, REGIONALISMS, NONSTANDARD ENGLISH

SLANG

Slang is the informal, colourful vocabulary that is often unique to and coined by subgroups such as teenagers, college students, musicians, skateboarders, computer programmers, street gangs, rap artists, and soldiers. Slang is often used to communicate the unique common experiences of these subgroups, and it is frequently not understood by all segments of society. Most often, slang attempts to be current and trendy, but such language is soon overused and quickly becomes dated. For instance, in the early part of the twentieth century, the expression *the cat's pyjamas* was the fashionable way to call something or someone *excellent*; more recently, a *cool dude* might use the slang terms *bad* and *wicked*. Other more modern examples of slang include *bummer*, *grunt*, *rip-off*, *wired*, or *preppie*.

Slang can often make story dialogue sound lively and authentic. However, it is inappropriate in formal writing such as academic essays and business letters.

> Jeff ~~flunked~~ failed his final history ~~exam,~~ examination and now his semester ~~is a~~ has been ~~total write-off~~ completely wasted.

Slang: Mel and her gang are coming over, and we're going to watch the tube and pig out.

Formal: Mel and her friends are coming over. We plan to watch television and eat snacks.

REGIONAL EXPRESSIONS

A regional expression is an expression that is common to a particular area of the country. For instance, in Atlantic Canada, a *barachois* is "a tidal pond partly obstructed by a bar" (*Nelson Canadian Dictionary*, p. 108).

Murray could see the skiff beyond the <u>barachois</u>.

Regional expressions, like slang, can add colour and authenticity; however, they may not be familiar to a general audience and should be avoided in formal academic writing.

After he caught the winning salmon, his competitors threw

the fisherman in the ~~salt chuck~~ *ocean*.

Salt chuck is a regional expression used in British Columbia and the U.S. Pacific Northwest. It might not be known to all Canadians.

Many Canadian dictionaries have notes indicating if a word or expression is regional.

NONSTANDARD ENGLISH

Nonstandard English is acceptable in informal social and regional contexts, but it should be avoided in any formal writing. Examples of nonstandard English include the following words and phrases from the Glossary of Usage:

> *anyways, bursted, nowheres,* and *theirselves.*

Standard English, on the other hand, is the written English commonly expected and used in educational institutions, businesses, government, and other contexts in which people must formally communicate with one another. Use standard English in all of your academic writing. If you are in doubt about whether a word or phrase is standard or nonstandard English, check in the Glossary of Usage in this handbook or in a good Canadian dictionary.

Nonstandard: The guy was nowheres in sight. He could of left town, but she didn't care anyways.

Standard: The man was nowhere in sight. He could have left town, but she did not care anyway.

LEVELS OF FORMALITY

Informal writing is casual in language and tone, and it is appropriate for communication in such forms as notes, friendly letters, e-mails to close friends, journal entries, and brief memorandums to people you know very well.

Formal writing is formal in tone and language, and it is appropriate for academic and business writing such as essays, research reports, job application letters, and business letters and reports.

When deciding which level of formality to use in a piece of writing, you should consider two key factors:

1. Subject
2. Audience

As you draft and revise your work, ask the following questions about the level of formality you select.

SUBJECT
- Is my choice of words appropriate to the seriousness of my subject?

AUDIENCE
- What type of language will my audience expect?
- Is my choice of words appropriate for the intended audience?
- Does my choice of words and the tone these words create make me seem too close or too distant from my readers?

In any academic or business writing you do, use a formal level of writing and assume a serious tone. The following opening line of a career application letter is too informal.

> ✕ I'm just dropping you a few lines to put my name in for that fisheries biologist's assistant job I saw somewhere in the *Free Press* a few weeks back.

> ✔ I am writing to apply for the fisheries biologist's assistant position advertised in the June 16 edition of the *Free Press*.

The level of language can also seem highly inappropriate when too formal.

Too Formal: When the illustrious Maple Leafs exited from the frozen playing surface trailing their less renowned opponents, the Wild, by the modest score of 1–0, the assembled spectators vigorously voiced their disapproval. The officials in charge of the National Hockey League were authentic demons for having the audacity to schedule these mismatched contests between the annual All-Star Game and the hockey tournament that is part of Olympic competition.

More Appropriate: When the Leafs left the ice trailing the Wild 1–0, a smattering of boos rained down from the crowd. The NHL was the real culprit for slipping lopsided games like these between the All-Star Game and the Olympics.

NONSEXIST LANGUAGE

Sexist language is biased in attributing characteristics and roles to people exclusively on the basis of gender. Sometimes sexist language is very obvious, but often it is less so. Sexist language can be explicit, as in calling an attractive young woman a *hot chick*. It can be patronizing by referring to a mature woman as a *girl Friday*. It can reflect stereotypical thinking by unnecessarily drawing attention to a person's gender, as in *a female university president*. And sexist language can be subtle, yet still highly biased, by including only male pronouns when more inclusive language is needed; for example, *an athlete always needs to maintain his composure*.

Sexist language can apply to men as well as women; for instance, if a writer describes *a male kindergarten teacher*.

There are a number of strategies you can use to avoid sexist language.

1. Treat all people equally in your descriptions of them.

    ✕ Mr. Delmonico, Mr. Habib, Mr. Dawson, and <u>Tillie, the secretary,</u> arrived for the meeting.

    ✔ Mr. Delmonico, Mr. Habib, Mr. Dawson, and <u>Ms. Lord</u> arrived for the meeting.

2. Avoid stereotypes.

    Stereotyping: Like all men, he hates to cook.

3. Use pairs of pronouns to indicate inclusive gender references.

    ✕ A professor is motivated by <u>his</u> students.

    ✔ A professor is motivated by <u>his or her</u> students.

4. Rewrite the sentence as a plural.

    ✔ <u>Professors</u> are motivated by <u>their</u> students.

5. Rewrite the sentence so there is no gender problem.

    ✔ <u>A professor</u> is motivated by <u>students</u>.

6. Make gender-neutral word choices.

AVOIDING SEXIST LANGUAGE

INAPPROPRIATE	GENDER-NEUTRAL
alderman	city council member, councillor
anchorman	anchor
businessman	businessperson, entrepreneur
chairman	chairperson, chair
clergyman	member of the clergy, minister
coed	student
craftsman	artisan, craftsperson
fireman	firefighter
forefather	ancestor
foreman	supervisor
freshman	first-year student
housewife	homemaker
mailman	mail carrier, letter carrier, postal worker
male nurse	nurse
mankind	people, humankind, human
manpower	personnel, human resources
newsman	journalist, reporter
policeman	police officer
salesman	salesperson, sales clerk
stewardess	flight attendant
to man	to staff, to operate
weatherman	weather forecaster
waitress	server
workman	worker, labourer, employee

PRECISION IN LANGUAGE

When trying to choose the most precise word to communicate your meaning, you may find a number of language reference books helpful. Among the most useful will be a good Canadian dictionary and a book of synonyms and antonyms such as *Roget's Thesaurus*, *Gage Canadian Thesaurus*, or *Fitzhenry and Whiteside's Canadian Thesaurus*.

CONNOTATIONS

Many words have two levels of meaning: a **denotative** meaning and a **connotative** meaning. The denotative meaning of a word is its common, literal, dictionary meaning. The connotative meaning is the emotional meaning of the word, which includes experiences and associations you make when you see a word in print or hear it spoken. For example, the dictionary meaning of *eagle* is "a large bird of prey." However, the word *eagle* also carries additional emotional and associative meanings such as "power," "pride," "majesty," and "fierceness."

When considering any word for a piece of writing, you should consider both its denotative and connotative meanings. Sometimes by using a word with certain connotations, you could imply a meaning you do not intend. Conversely, you can enhance your intended meaning by selecting the word with the most appropriate connotations for your subject, purpose, and audience. Often, reviewing all listed meanings in a dictionary entry will give you a sense of a word's connotations. Take special care when using a thesaurus to be sensitive to the connotations of a word. For example, *dissipated* means "scattered" when applied to clouds, but "drunken or disorderly" when applied to people. Context affects connotation and can profoundly affect meaning.

> laughed
> The young women ~~giggled~~ at all the right parts of the Restoration comedy.

Giggled has an association with immaturity, and since the women were *young*, the sentence implies the women were immature. The intended meaning of the sentence was that the women appreciated the humour of the play, so *laughed* is more appropriate.

> has   had
> Ethel ~~is a victim of~~ rheumatoid arthritis and has ~~suffered from~~ it for ten years.

It would be even better to use this sentence instead: *Ethel was diagnosed with rheumatoid arthritis ten years ago.* Other emotional language related to suffering is best avoided since this kind of language adds an inappropriate slant to the meaning.

CONCRETE NOUNS

There are many types of nouns.

GENERAL AND SPECIFIC NOUNS

Nouns can be very general or very specific. Suppose a friend asks, *What did you do on Saturday?* You respond: *I watched a comedy. Comedy* is a very broad, general noun. Your response could refer to a sophisticated Shakespearean comedy, a television situation comedy, or a particular movie, such as *Ace Ventura, Pet Detective*. All of these individual alternatives within the general category comedy are specific nouns.

ABSTRACT AND CONCRETE NOUNS

Nouns can be abstract or concrete. Abstract nouns refer to concepts, ideas, qualities, and conditions. Examples include *love, charity, kindness, humanism, youth,* and *integrity*. Concrete nouns name things that are detectable by your senses, such as *snake, dill, sunset, coffee, caramel,* and *harp*.

Many professional creative writers, especially poets and novelists, spend a great deal of time selecting the most appropriate and precise word to communicate an idea or feeling. Similarly, in your own writing, try to select the most effective word for your writing purpose. Of course, in the range of your writing assignments, you will frequently need to describe, explain, and evaluate general and abstract content. At these times, general and abstract language will be most appropriate. But wherever possible, use specific and concrete nouns to make your writing clear and evocative.

~~Hazy city air~~ Toronto's smog made it difficult to breathe as we ~~put the boat~~ launched the sailboat ~~in the water~~ onto Lake Ontario.

General abstract nouns, such as *things, considerations,* and *aspects,* are extremely vague and lacking in colour.

We plan to ~~do a number of things~~ have several renovations done to improve our home.

There are several ~~considerations to be addressed~~ issues to discuss before we allow the new subdivision.

ACTIVE VERBS

Where possible, choose precise verbs that give your writing impact and power.

WHICH VERBS ARE WEAK?
Weak verbs are forms of the verb *be* (*be, am, is, are, was, were, being, been*). None of these verb forms communicates a specific action. As well, verbs in the passive voice tend to be lacking in power and can lead to lifeless, uninspiring writing: *An acceptable job was done by her.*

HOW CAN I USE VERBS TO MAKE MY WRITING LIVELY?
Choose precise, vigorous, emphatic, expressive, or descriptive verbs in the active voice. In the following examples, the sentence has been revised from one that uses the verb *be* in the passive voice to a precise verb in the active voice.

> *Passive Voice:* The eager young actors *were trained* by the dynamic acting coach.

> *Active Voice:* The dynamic acting coach *trained* the eager young actors.

Use the most precise and descriptive verbs to communicate vividly the action(s) performed in your sentence.

> As she ~~got near to~~ approached the finish line, the marathon runner ~~leaned toward~~ lunged for the tape, ~~crinkled her face~~ grimaced, and ~~fell down~~ collapsed.

WHEN SHOULD I REPLACE THE VERB BE?
Change the form of the verb *be* when it creates a wordy construction.

> Keeping the prisoners in cages would ~~be an infringement of~~ infringe on their human rights.

Using the verb *infringe* is more dynamic—and more economical—than using *be an infringement of.*

WHEN SHOULD I NOT REPLACE THE VERB BE?
Keep forms of the verb *be* in the following circumstances:

- when you want to link the subject of a sentence with a noun that renames the subject or an adjective that describes it

  Life *is* a bed of roses.

Bed-and-breakfast proprietors *are* usually hospitable.

- when they function as helping verbs before present participles

  The elk *are* vanishing.

- when expressing ongoing action

  I was driving to work when I heard that several buildings *were* burning in the downtown core.

WHEN SHOULD I REPLACE A PASSIVE VERB?

With sentences in the active voice, the subject performs the action.

Active Voice: José *hammered* the nail.

With sentences in the passive voice, the subject receives the action.

Passive Voice: The nail *was hammered* by José.

In some passive sentences the performer of the action is not mentioned.

The nail *was hammered*.

Strong writing clearly states who or what performs the action. Use the active voice by making the person or thing that performs the action the subject of the sentence.

The class selected
ₐ "Canada's Ethnic Diversity" ~~was selected by the class~~ as the theme for the panel discussion.

WHEN SHOULD I NOT REPLACE A PASSIVE VERB?

Use the passive voice in the following situations:

- when you want to emphasize who or what receives the action
- when you want to give less emphasis to the person or thing performing the action
- when the person or thing performing the action is not known

For example, in the example involving José and the nail (above), you would choose the active voice if you wished to emphasize José's importance. If you wanted to emphasize the importance of the nail being hammered, you would use the passive voice. And if hammering the nail was of central importance and José of no importance whatsoever, or you didn't know who did the hammering, you would use *The nail was hammered.*

MISUSED WORDS

When working on a draft, you may want to use a word but may be unsure of the word's meaning or spelling. Always check the meaning of such words in a good dictionary. Misusing words can confuse your overall meaning and create unintentional humour.

conscious
Burns is ~~conscience~~ of his own powers of destruction.

censored
The provincial review committee ~~censured~~ the pornographic movie.

cited
In a definitive book on Gorbachev, the author ~~sighted~~ the main reasons for the collapse of the Soviet Union.

Many writers incorrectly use a noun when the meaning and sentence structure require an adjective. For instance, they might use *abhorrence*, *indulgence*, or *independence* in sentences that require the adjective forms *abhorrent*, *indulgent*, or *independent*, respectively.

abhorrent
It is an ~~abhorrence~~ practice when advertisers target viewers under five years of age.

STANDARD IDIOMS

An idiom is an expression whose meaning can't be determined by simply knowing the definition of each word within the idiom. Many idioms are very colourful and easy to spot: *kill two birds with one stone, read between the lines, the last straw.*

An idiom always appears in one particular form, one that may not necessarily be taken literally. An example of an idiom is *beside himself* [or *herself*]. *She was beside herself* means "She was in a state of extreme excitement or agitation."

Using idiomatic expressions with prepositions can be tricky. An unidiomatic expression may make better literal sense, but the idiomatic expression is used because it is accepted English usage. If you are in doubt, check a good Canadian dictionary by looking up the word before the preposition.

AVOIDING UNIDIOMATIC EXPRESSIONS

UNIDIOMATIC	IDIOMATIC
according with	according to
angry at	angry with
capable to	capable of
comply to	comply with
desirous to	desirous of
different than	different from
go by	go to
intend on doing	intend to do
off of	off
plan on doing	plan to do
preferable than	preferable to
prior than	prior to
recommend her to do	recommend that she do
superior than	superior to
sure and	sure to
try and	try to
type of a	type of
wait on a person	wait for a person
wait on line	wait in line
with reference in	with reference to

CLICHÉS

A **cliché** is an overused phrase or expression that has become tired and predictable and, hence, is ineffective for freshly communicating writing ideas.

SELECTED CLICHÉS TO AVOID IN YOUR WRITING		
add insult to injury	easier said than done	in the long run
at long last	few and far between	in this day and age
a word to the wise	finishing touches	it stands to reason
cool as a cucumber	first and foremost	narrow escape
cold as ice	good as gold	red-letter day

You might wish to create a computer file of these and other clichés to avoid.

Clichés, by being so predictable, deprive writing of any sense of surprise. However, in some rare instances, you might inject freshness into a cliché by giving it an unexpected twist.

He is as strong as an ox; unfortunately, that describes his odour, too.

FIGURES OF SPEECH

In figurative language, words carry more than their literal meaning. **Figures of speech** are particular types of figurative language. Common examples of figures of speech are **similes**, **personification**, and **metaphors**. In a simile, a comparison is made between two different ideas or objects, using *like* or *as*. In personification, human traits are assigned to something that is not human. And in a metaphor, a comparison is made between two otherwise dissimilar ideas or objects; here, the comparison does not use *like* or *as*.

Used effectively, figures of speech can add colour and emphasis to your writing and enrich meaning. However, used without care, they can make writing clumsy. A common writing problem is mixing metaphors. In a **mixed** metaphor, two or more incongruous images are mingled.

keep focus while
She was able to ~~take a firm foothold~~ in the eye of public opinion.

Harry   depth of depression
~~The Grand Canyon of Harry's depression~~ reached the ~~pinnacle~~ when his pet died.

PUNCTUATION
punctuation

" All morning I worked on the proof of one of my poems, and I took out a comma; in the afternoon I put it back. "

—OSCAR WILDE

PUNCTUATION

This section on punctuation follows the one on grammar because so many issues of punctuation depend on a knowledge of how the language is put together grammatically. For this reason, grammar checkers cannot easily catch routine comma errors, so don't rely on them to do so. Refer to this section for advice on problem areas you encounter as you compose and revise.

The Comma

Frequently, a comma is essential to ensure that readers clearly understand your intended meaning. Omitting or misplacing a comma can easily lead to misreadings.

> While e-mailing‸ Mary Beth spoke on the telephone with her stockbroker.

Without the comma, this sentence could be interpreted to mean that Beth was speaking on the phone with her stockbroker while e-mailing Mary.

The following sections provide rules and guidance for instances in which you must use commas.

INDEPENDENT CLAUSES WITH A COORDINATING CONJUNCTION

In some sentences, two or more independent clauses (clauses that can stand on their own as sentences) are linked by coordinating conjunctions (*and, or, for, but, so, nor,* and *yet*). In such sentences, place a comma before the coordinating conjunction.

> <u>I enjoy watching television</u>, but <u>I draw the line at World Wrestling Entertainment</u>.

Exception: If the two independent clauses are very short, and there is no chance of misinterpreting the sentence, the comma may be omitted.

> <u>The Greyhound bus pulled in</u> and we boarded it.

INTRODUCTORY ELEMENTS

COMMAS WITH INTRODUCTORY ADVERBIAL CLAUSES
An introductory adverbial clause is a construction that has a subject and a verb and that introduces a main clause.

> <u>Whenever I feel in need of cheering up,</u> I go to the park.

Introductory adverbial clauses indicate *where, when, why, how,* or *under what conditions* the main sentence action takes place. After such clauses, use a comma to indicate that the main part of the sentence is about to start.

> Whenever he hears gossip about company plans for hiring‸ Pedro talks about his conspiracy theory.

> By a bend in the mighty Thompson River‸ I learned to swim.

If the adverbial phrase or clause is very brief, and there is no danger of misreading the sentence, the comma may be omitted.

> In a flash it was over.

COMMAS WITH LONGER INTRODUCTORY PREPOSITIONAL PHRASES

After longer introductory prepositional phrases, use a comma to indicate that the main part of the sentence is about to start.

> After appetizers and an extended family dinner‸ my uncle fell asleep in his chair.

ITEMS IN A SERIES

A series in a sentence can be made up of three or more words, phrases, or clauses that have the same grammatical form and are of equal importance. Place commas between the items in the series (e.g., *knife, fork, and spoon*). The comma before the last item, commonly called "the serial comma," is optional, and it is omitted by many writers. However, the serial comma is useful in preventing ambiguity. If you decide to use the serial comma, make sure that you use it consistently throughout your writing.

> Serena thanked her parents, Karen Kain‸ and Frank Augustyn, for helping her win the award for her dancing.

Without the serial comma, it is unclear: are Serena's parents Karen Kain and Frank Augustyn? With the serial comma, it is clear that she is thanking four different people.

> The woods are lovely, dark and deep.

The above line is from the famous Robert Frost poem "Stopping by Woods on a Snowy Evening." Here the punctuation is intentionally ambiguous. The speaker could mean that he considers the woods lovely because they are dark and deep, or that the woods are lovely *and* dark *and* deep.

Especially when writing a report or essay, it is wise to use the comma between all elements in a series to avoid any possibility of ambiguity or misinterpretation by the reader.

Note: Do not place a comma *before the first* or *after the last* item in a series, unless another comma rule makes using a comma necessary.

> The poets E.J. Pratt, F.R. Scott, and A.J.M. Smith played an important role in the development of uniquely Canadian poetry.

> There were two bars of soap, a box of detergent, some hamburger buns, and onions in her shopping cart.

COORDINATE ADJECTIVES

Coordinate adjectives are two or more adjectives that separately and equally modify a noun or pronoun. The order of these adjectives can be changed without affecting the meaning of the sentence. Coordinate adjectives can be joined by *and*. Separate coordinate adjectives with commas.

> The cold, smelly, wet basement was off-limits to the children as a play area.

> It was a fluffy playful tiny kitten.

You can tell these adjectives are coordinate since they can easily be linked with *and* (*cold* and *smelly* and *wet*).

CUMULATIVE ADJECTIVES

A **cumulative** adjective modifies the adjective that comes after it and the noun or pronoun that follows. Cumulative adjectives increase meaning from word to word as they progress toward a noun or pronoun. They are not interchangeable and cannot be joined by *and*. Do not use a comma between cumulative adjectives.

> The book talk featured three well-known English authors.

English modifies *authors*, *well-known* modifies *English authors*, and *three* modifies *well-known English authors*. The order of the adjectives cannot be changed, nor can the coordinating conjunction *and* be placed between the adjectives.

> His résumé included various short-term landscaping jobs.

> An exhibit of authentic early Incan art was on display at the Royal Ontario Museum.

> The music festival featured many Canadian folk acts.

RESTRICTIVE AND NONRESTRICTIVE ELEMENTS

Adjective clauses, adjective phrases, and appositives can modify nouns and pronouns. These modifying elements may be either restrictive or nonrestrictive.

WHAT IS A RESTRICTIVE ELEMENT?

A **restrictive** element limits, defines, or identifies the noun or pronoun that it modifies. The information in a restrictive element is essential to a sentence's meaning. Do not set off a restrictive element with commas.

> The man <u>who has the scar above his left eyebrow</u> is the chief robbery suspect.

The fact that the man has a scar is essential to identifying him as the chief robbery suspect. Omitting the restrictive element would greatly alter the meaning of the sentence, turning it into a very general statement.

WHAT IS A NONRESTRICTIVE ELEMENT?

A **nonrestrictive** element adds nonessential, or parenthetical, information about an idea or term that is already limited, defined, or identified; hence, a nonrestrictive element is set off with a comma or commas.

> The man has a scar, <u>which is above his left eyebrow</u>.

The essential meaning of the sentence—that the man has a scar—is not lost if the information about the location of the scar is removed; thus, this information is nonrestrictive.

CONCLUDING ADVERB CLAUSES

Adverb clauses introducing a sentence almost always conclude with a comma. (See page 72.) However, when adverb clauses conclude a sentence and their meaning is essential to the sentence, they are not set off by commas. Adverb clauses that begin with the following subordinated conjunctions are usually essential: *after, as soon as, before, because, if, since, unless, until,* and *when.*

> Water boils at sea level <u>when it reaches a temperature of 100 degrees Celsius</u>.

The concluding adverb clause commencing with *when* is essential to the meaning of the sentence, so it is not set off with a comma.

Place a comma before adverb clauses that contain non-essential information. Adverb clauses beginning with the subordinating conjunctions *although*, *even though*, *though*, and *whereas* are often nonessential.

> He missed the turn for the expressway, <u>even though signs for the on-ramp were well posted</u>.

TRANSITIONS, PARENTHETICAL EXPRESSIONS, ABSOLUTE PHRASES, CONTRASTS

TRANSITIONAL EXPRESSIONS

Transitional expressions are words or groups of words that function as links between or within sentences. A transitional expression can appear at the beginning, end, or within a sentence. Transitional expressions can be conjunctive adverbs, such as *therefore* and *however*, or transitional phrases, such as *for example*, *in addition*, and *on the contrary*. (For a more complete list, see pages 80–81.)

If a transitional expression appears between independent clauses in a compound sentence, place a semicolon before the transitional expression. Most often, you should also place a comma after it.

> Edwin did not fit in with our crowd; <u>furthermore,</u> he was openly antagonistic toward us.

> The soprano was a prima donna; <u>for instance,</u> she demanded that mineral water chilled to a specific temperature be available in her dressing room before and after every performance.

Set off a transitional expression with commas if it appears at the start of a sentence or in the middle of an independent clause.

> <u>As a result</u>⌄ the medical insurance plan will not pay for liposuction.

> The dermatologist comes highly recommended; he can't give me an appointment⌄ however⌄ until the end of March.

In some cases, if the transitional expression is integrated with the sentence and requires no pause or a minimal one when reading, no commas are needed to set off the expression. Expressions such as the following may not always need to be set off by commas:

> *at least, certainly, consequently, indeed, of course, perhaps, then, therefore, undoubtedly*

> You have been a good child; <u>therefore</u> you will get a pet pony.

The Drowsy Chaperone is a Canadian musical; <u>indeed</u>, it was created and staged in Toronto some years before it appeared on Broadway in 2006.

PARENTHETICAL EXPRESSIONS

Parenthetical expressions contain additional information the writer inserts into the sentence for such purposes as to explain, qualify, or give his or her point of view. If parenthetical expressions do not appear in parentheses, they are set off with commas.

The inarticulate politician, <u>unfortunately</u>, stated his contra-dictory views about abortion on national television.

In most writing situations, <u>such as this one</u>, commas are used to set off parenthetical expressions.

While commas are required to set off *distinctly* parenthetical expressions, do *not* use commas to set off *mildly* parenthetical expressions.

Team Canada finally scored the winning goal.

ABSOLUTE PHRASES

An absolute phrase contains a noun subject and a participle that modify an entire sentence. Set off absolute phrases with commas.

<u>The war being over</u>, the refugees returned home.

<u>Their profits steeply declining</u>, many computer companies laid off employees.

EXPRESSIONS OF CONTRAST

Expressions of contrast include words such as *not*, *nor*, *but*, and *unlike*. Set off expressions of contrast with commas.

The Toronto Raptors, <u>unlike the Vancouver Grizzlies</u>, flour-ished in Canada.

Martin found fame as a standup comedian, <u>not as a writer</u>.

NOUNS OF DIRECT ADDRESS, *YES* AND *NO*, INTERROGATIVE TAGS, INTERJECTIONS

Use commas to set off the following:

- nouns of direct address

Your backflip, <u>Olga</u>, is of Olympic calibre.

- the words *yes* and *no*

  No⌃ you don't sound crazy.

- interrogative tags

  You did turn off the iron⌃ didn't you?

- mild interjections

  Of course⌃ incidents like that are inevitable.

HE SAID, ETC.

Use commas with speech tags such as *she wrote* or *he said* to set off direct quotations. (See also page 92.)

Woody Allen wrote⌃ "It is impossible to experience one's death objectively and still carry a tune."

"Defining and analyzing humor is a pastime of humorless people⌃ " quipped Robert Benchley.

DATES, ADDRESSES, TITLES, NUMBERS

DATES
When the date is within the sentence, use commas following the day and the year in month-day-year dates.

On August 14⌃ 1945⌃ Japan surrendered.

When the date is inverted or when just the month and year are given, commas are not required.

Queen Victoria's birthday will be celebrated on 21 May 2007.

January 2002 was unseasonably warm.

ADDRESSES
Use a comma between the city and province or city and country. When a sentence continues on after the city and province or city and country, also use a comma after the province or country.

Stephen Leacock died in Toronto⌃ Ontario⌃ in 1944.

In a complete address, separate all items (except the postal code) with a comma.

I would appreciate it if you would courier the book to Ella James at 126 Mayburn Drive⌃ Oakville⌃ Ontario L6P 1K8.

TITLES

When an abbreviated title follows a name, place a comma after the name and a second comma after the title.

Philip Bacho⌃ Ph.D.⌃ taught the course on writing scripts.

NUMBERS

Canada follows the international system of metric measurement (SI), which does not use commas in numbers. Instead, spaces are used to separate sets of three digits. Four-digit numbers may be grouped together. Be aware that many U.S. style guides use the imperial system instead and hence do not conform to the international system of metric measurement.

In your reading, you may encounter commas used for numbers that are four digits or more. This system was used before Canada adopted the international metric system.

4673   233 971   6,299,381

Never use commas to separate sets of digits in years, telephone numbers, street numbers, or postal codes.

PREVENTING CONFUSION

In many writing situations, commas are required to prevent reader confusion.

OMITTED WORDS

A comma is used to indicate that an understood word or words have been omitted.

Tasha adored jazz; Bert⌃ gospel.

ECHOING WORDS

When two words repeat or strongly echo each other, a comma helps to clarify sentence meaning.

Undeterred by the possibility of plane hijackings, he felt that whatever happens⌃ happens.

CLARIFYING A WRITER'S INTENTION

Occasionally commas are required to help readers group units of meaning as the writer intended.

Those who can⌃ run every chance they get.

The Semicolon

A semicolon is used to separate major elements of a sentence that are of equal grammatical rank.

INDEPENDENT CLAUSES WITH NO COORDINATING CONJUNCTION

An independent clause expresses a complete thought and can stand on its own as a sentence. When related independent clauses appear in a sentence (as in a compound sentence), they are usually linked by a comma and a coordinating conjunction (*and, but, for, nor, or, so,* and *yet*). The conjunction indicates the relationship between the clauses.

When the relationship between independent clauses is clear without the conjunction, you may instead link the two clauses with a semicolon.

> A teacher affects eternity; no one can tell where his influence stops.
>
> —Henry Adams

Use a semicolon if a coordinating conjunction between two independent clauses has been omitted. If you use a comma, you will create a grammatical error known as a comma splice.

> Provincial health insurance plans cover some medical costs when Canadians travel outside the country; they do not cover many vital health-care expenses.

Strategies for revising comma splice errors can be found on pages 8–10. You may wish to consider other alternatives to using a semicolon.

INDEPENDENT CLAUSES WITH TRANSITIONAL EXPRESSIONS

Transitional expressions can be conjunctive adverbs or transitional phrases.

TRANSITIONAL EXPRESSIONS

Common Conjunctive Adverbs
accordingly, also, anyway, besides, certainly, consequently, conversely, finally, further, furthermore, hence, however, incidentally, indeed, instead, likewise, meanwhile, moreover, namely, nevertheless, next, nonetheless, now, otherwise, similarly, specifically, still, subsequently, then, thereafter, therefore, thus, undoubtedly

Transitional Phrases
after all, as a matter of fact, as a result, as an illustration, at any rate, at the same time, equally important, even so, for example, for instance, in addition, in conclusion, in fact, in other words, in short, in spite of, in summary, in the first place, in the same way, of course, on the contrary, on the other hand, to be sure, to illustrate

When a transitional expression comes between independent clauses, place a semicolon before the expression and a comma after it.

> She is an authority on the West Nile virus; <u>furthermore</u>, we need someone with her expertise.

If the transitional expression is in the middle of or at the end of the second independent clause, the semicolon is placed between the independent clauses.

> Generally people who work at the biological station have advanced postsecondary degrees; Tony, <u>on the other hand</u>, acquired his knowledge and expertise through practical experience.

Do not confuse the punctuation for transitional expressions with that used with coordinating conjunctions (*and, but, for, nor, or, so,* and *yet*). When a coordinating conjunction links two independent clauses, it is preceded by a comma. (See pages 8–9 and 72.)

SERIES WITH INTERNAL PUNCTUATION

Usually, commas separate items in a series. However, when series items contain commas, a semicolon is placed between items to make the sentence easier to read.

> Here is the list of remaining speakers and topics: Gurdeep, the rewards of working at a student newspaper; Miles, the elements of hip-hop; and Mustapha, the wonders of wireless technology.

Without semicolons, the sentence would be difficult to read. In each series element, the speaker's name is followed by the topic of his speech. The semicolons help the reader to group information accurately.

INCORRECT USES OF THE SEMICOLON

Never use a semicolon in the following writing situations:

- between independent clauses joined by *and, but, for, nor, or, so,* or *yet*

  lifetime, yet
  The painter was very prolific during his ~~lifetime; yet~~ he achieved the fame he deserved only after death.

- between a subordinate clause and the remainder of the sentence

  lemon curd, Leona
  After she had made the ~~lemon curd; Leona~~ whipped the cream she needed to ice the cake.

The Semicolon

- between an appositive and the word to which it refers

  Life, a

  Raj's favourite television program is ~~*Life; a*~~ dark but funny dramatic series.

- to introduce a list

  course: Bleak

  A number of great novels are covered in the ~~course; *Bleak*~~ *House, Pride and Prejudice,* and *Gulliver's Travels.*

The Colon

The colon is most often used as a formal and emphatic method to introduce a word, phrase, or clause that follows it.

BEFORE A LIST, AN APPOSITIVE, A QUOTATION

Use a colon before

- a list

  For this experiment, you will need the following materials: <u>three small cups, a transparent sheet, a waterproof marker, an eye dropper, and three paper towels.</u>

- an appositive

  While held hostage, the journalist had one all-consuming thought: <u>survival.</u>

- a quotation

  Mackenzie King summed up his position with this epigrammatic line: <u>"Not necessarily conscription, but conscription if necessary."</u>

For additional ways of introducing quotations, see pages 91–92.

BETWEEN INDEPENDENT CLAUSES

You can use either a capital letter or a lowercase letter to begin the independent clause after the colon.

  In North America, there are two classes of travel: there is first-class travel, and then there is travel with children.

CONVENTIONAL USES

The colon is conventionally used

- after the salutation of a formal letter

  Dear Ms. Pointman:

- to indicate hours and minutes

  6:31 a.m.

- between numbers in ratios

  The ratio of men over fifty was 5:1.

- between the title and subtitle of a book

  Dancing at the Edge of the World: Thoughts on Words, Women, Places

- to separate the city from the publisher and date in a bibliographic entry

  Toronto: Nelson, 2006.

- between Bible chapters and verses

  Psalms 23:1–3

INCORRECT USES OF THE COLON

Except in documentation, a complete independent clause must precede a colon.

Do not use a colon in the following writing situations:

- between a verb and its complement or object

  The main ingredients in a good mushroom omelette are: eggs, mushrooms, and butter.

- between a preposition and its object

  The open-area portion of the dome house consisted of: a kitchen, living room, and master bedroom.

- after *for example, such as,* and *including/included*

  The content of the botanist's lecture included: boreal forests, a Carolinian forest, and an Amazonian rain forest.

Note, too, that it is optional to capitalize after a colon if what follows is an independent clause. If what follows is not an independent clause, do not capitalize.

The Apostrophe

POSSESSIVE NOUNS

An apostrophe (') appears as part of a noun to indicate that the word is possessive. Often ownership is obvious, as in *Mishka's hockey stick* or *the instructor's briefcase*. Sometimes ownership is not as explicit, as in *the journey's end* or *the river's tributaries*. To test if a noun is possessive, see if you can state it as an "of" phrase, as in *the end of the journey* or *the tributaries of the river*. According to this test, both nouns, *journey's* and *river's*, are possessive.

POSSESSIVES FORMED BY ADDING AN APOSTROPHE AND -S

- a singular or plural noun that does not end in -*s*

   The <u>commodore's</u> cabin cruiser ran aground.

   It was the <u>team's</u> wish that the donation be made in his name.

   The <u>women's</u> shelter needs volunteers.

- a singular noun that ends in -*s*.

   <u>Gus's</u> father owns a single-engine plane.

Exception: For names such as Moses and Jesus, or if the noun ends in an "eez" sound, an apostrophe without an -*s* may be added to a singular noun. (You may see this usage with other nouns ending in -*s*; however, the preferred style is to add an apostrophe and -*s* as shown above.)

   <u>Euripides'</u> tragedy *Medea* is his best-known work.

POSSESSIVES FORMED BY ADDING AN APOSTROPHE ONLY

- The noun is plural and ends in -*s*.

   <u>Workers'</u> rights were neglected by the military regime.

   The <u>boys'</u> tent was flattened in the storm.

WITH COMPOUND SUBJECTS

To show joint possession, use -'*s* (or -*s*') with the last noun only.

   You should see <u>Doug and Dino's</u> modified stock car.

   <u>Manuela and Jesus'</u> new house overlooks the valley.

To show individual possession, make all nouns in the compound subject possessive.

   <u>Todd's</u> and <u>Charles's</u> ideas on how to decorate the home were diametrically opposed.

WITH COMPOUND NOUNS

Use -'*s* (or -*s*') with the last element in a compound noun to show possession.

   My sister-in-<u>law's</u> film won a Genie.

   My in-<u>laws'</u> parties are always worth attending.

POSSESSIVE INDEFINITE PRONOUNS

An indefinite pronoun refers to a general or non-specific person or thing. Examples of indefinite pronouns are *somebody, anything,* and *anyone.* Add -'s to the end of the indefinite pronoun to make it possessive.

It is not <u>anybody's</u> business what I do in my free time.

<u>Someone's</u> laptop was stolen from the reference library.

CONTRACTIONS

The apostrophe takes the place of missing letters in contractions.

<u>Who's</u> going to do it <u>doesn't</u> matter.

Who's written in full is *Who is,* and *doesn't* written in full is *does not.*

The apostrophe can also indicate that the first two digits of years have been left out.

There will be a reunion for the class of <u>'88</u>.

Note that, when referring to a decade, the plural is formed by adding -s (no apostrophe) after the year. Be careful to use the apostrophe correctly when dealing with decades in your writing.

She lived in Paris in the <u>1940s</u>.

Did you enjoy *That '70s Show*?

PLURALS OF NUMBERS, LETTERS, ETC.

In some common writing situations, an apostrophe plus -s is used to form the plural.

- numbers

  As scores for his perfect dive, he received all <u>10's</u>.

- letters

  Tiny <u>X's</u> and <u>O's</u> were embroidered on the scarf.

- word as words

  I don't want to have to deal with any more <u>*what if*'s</u>.

- abbreviations

  It was the responsibility of the Calgary-area <u>M.P.'s</u> to ensure the issue was addressed.

Notice that the -s is not italicized when used with italicized words or letters.

You should also note that some style guides (e.g., that of the Modern Language Association) do not use an apostrophe to form the plurals of numbers and abbreviations. Ask your instructor if there is a preferred style for your discipline.

He has trouble writing 6s. [MLA style]

I bought some new DVDs. [MLA style]

INCORRECT USES OF THE APOSTROPHE

Do not use an apostrophe with the following:

- nouns that are not possessive

  Employee's must wear security badges at all times.

  The clients' had expected us to pick up the tab for dinner.

- the possessive pronouns *his, hers, its, ours, theirs,* and *whose*

  The dog must wear it's collar when outdoors.

Here, *its* must be the possessive, so there is no apostrophe needed. Do not mistake the contraction *it's* ("it is") for the possessive *its*.

Quotation Marks

DIRECT QUOTATIONS

Direct quotations are the exact words copied from a print source or transcribed from what a person says. Direct quotations must be enclosed within quotation marks.

"The open ocean is normally a friendly environment for a sea kayak," writes John Dowd in *Sea Kayaking: A Manual for Long-Distance Touring.*

On the other hand, indirect quotations paraphrase or summarize what has appeared in a print source or what a person has said. Indirect quotations are not placed within quotation marks.

John Dowd professes that, usually, the open ocean is a safe place to sea kayak.

QUOTING LONGER PASSAGES BY A SINGLE SPEAKER
If you are directly quoting passages by a single speaker, start each new paragraph with quotation marks, but do not use closing quotation marks until the end of the quoted material.

MARKING A CHANGE IN SPEAKER WITHIN DIALOGUE

Start a new paragraph to signal a change in the speaker.

> "I said me, not you."
>
> "Oh. You got a car outside?"
>
> "I can walk."
>
> "That's five miles back to where the van is."
>
> "People have walked five miles."
>
> —Alice Munro, "Friend of My Youth"
> in Friend of My Youth (Toronto: McClelland & Stewart,
> 1990).

LONG QUOTATIONS

PROSE

A "long" quotation of prose is any passage that is more than four typed or handwritten lines. Start the quotation 2.5 cm (1 in.) from the left margin. You do not need to enclose the longer quotation within quotation marks because the indented format establishes for the reader that the quotation is taken exactly from a source. Usually, longer quotations are introduced by a sentence ending with a colon.

Smoking can destroy the health of smokers and is a very real health risk to those around them, as researcher Warren Clark clearly points out:

> In 1995, 4.5 million nonsmoking Canadians aged 15 and over were exposed to cigarette smoke on a daily basis. Another 2.2 million were exposed to it at least once a week, while about 840 000 were exposed to it less frequently. In terms of percentages, about 28 per cent of nonsmokers aged 15 and over breathed secondhand smoke every day, while about 19 per cent were exposed to it somewhat less often. Just over half of nonsmokers reported that they were not exposed to ETS (Environmental Tobacco Smoke). (161)

Placing the page number reference within parentheses follows the citation style prescribed by the Modern Language Association. (See page 114.)

If the direct quotation had included additional paragraphs, each new paragraph would need to be indented an additional 0.75 cm (0.3 in.).

POETRY

A "long" quotation of poetry is more than three lines of the poem. Start the quotation 2.5 cm (1 in.) from the left margin. You do not need to enclose the longer quotation within quotation marks because the indented format establishes for the reader that the quotation is taken exactly from the poem. Use quotation marks within the quotation only if they are part of the poem. (For information on how to punctuate two or three lines of poetry, see page 98.)

> P.K. Page is more personal in "After Rain" than in "The Stenographers." In "After Rain," she defines her own poetic sensibility through the poem-within-a-poem of stanza three:
>
>> the clothes-reel gauche
>>
>> as the rangy skeleton of some
>>
>> gaunt delicate spidery mute
>>
>> is pitched as if
>>
>> listening;
>>
>> while hung from one thin rib
>>
>> a silver web—
>>
>> its infant, skeletal, diminutive,
>>
>> now sagged with sequins, pulled ellipsoid,
>>
>> glistening. (122)

See MLA guidelines on how to include the reference in a Works Cited page. If your paper is written according to the style of the American Psychological Association, you will need to follow slightly different guidelines for setting off long quotations (see page 155).

QUOTATIONS WITHIN QUOTATIONS

Single quotation marks are used only to enclose quotations within quotations. Some confusion arises because this is a North American convention; British usage is the reverse (i.e., single quotation marks are the norm, and double quotation marks are used only inside single quotation marks).

> According to Newman et al., Charles de Gaulle "spoke the words that jolted a nation: 'Vive le Québec libre!'"

Two different quotation marks appear at the end of the quotation. The single quotation mark completes the interior quotation, while the double quotation mark completes the main quotation.

TITLES

Use quotation marks around titles of works that are included within other works, such as poems, short stories, newspaper and magazine articles, radio programs, television episodes, and chapters and other subdivisions of books.

> His talk focused on point of view in Edgar Allan Poe's short story "The Tell-Tale Heart."

The titles of plays, books, and films and the names of magazines should be set in italics if you are typing your manuscript. (Underline them if your manuscript is handwritten.)

WORDS AS WORDS

Italics or underlining is preferred for setting off words used as words. However, it is also acceptable to use quotation marks for this purpose.

> I remember once displaying my ignorance by using the word *irregardless* when I should have used *regardless*.

> I remember once displaying my ignorance by using the word "irregardless" when I should have used "regardless."

Note that double—not single—quotation marks are used.

WITH OTHER PUNCTUATION

The following section provides rules for using punctuation with quotation marks.

COMMAS AND PERIODS

Place commas and periods inside quotation marks. (Note that this is a North American convention; British usage generally places commas and periods outside quotation marks.)

"I'm not finished yet," she said. "The books I looked at were of no help."

Also follow the above punctuation rule in the following cases:

- with single quotation marks
- for titles of works
- for words used as words

Exception: If you follow Modern Language Association style guidelines for your paper, for parenthetical in-text citations, the period follows the final parenthesis. In this case, the period is therefore outside the quotation marks.

> Clarkson and McCall contend "Davis was apprehensive that Trudeau's pugnacity might scupper the possibility" (368).

SEMICOLONS AND COLONS
Place semicolons and colons outside quotation marks.

> He explained his term "in the moment": the individual focuses himself or herself on the elusive present.

> As the bank's head economist, she asserts that the economy will soon "take off"; several of her colleagues at other banks strongly disagree.

QUESTION MARKS AND EXCLAMATION MARKS
If the question mark or exclamation mark is part of the quoted material, place the question mark or exclamation mark *inside* the quotation marks.

PART OF THE QUOTED MATERIAL
> When Parminder heard what Susan had done, he shouted, "She made the shot from centre court!"

If the question mark or exclamation mark applies to the entire sentence, place a question mark or exclamation mark *outside* the quotation marks.

APPLIES TO THE ENTIRE SENTENCE
> What do you think of Napoleon's view that "history is a set of lies agreed upon"?

According to MLA style, the question mark or exclamation mark is placed before the final closing quotation mark; a sentence period is then placed after the final parenthesis in the parenthetical citation.

> Oliver Sacks ponders, "If this was the case in Virgil, what might happen if visual function was suddenly made possible, demanded?" (291).

INTRODUCING QUOTED MATERIAL

You have three major punctuation options when using a group of words to introduce a quotation:

1. a colon
2. a comma
3. no punctuation

WHEN TO USE THE COLON
Use the colon if the quotation has been formally introduced. A formal introduction is a complete independent clause.

> <u>In the *Globe and Mail,* John Stackhouse presents the following insight about political change in Africa:</u> "The economic revolution that has swept through Africa, from the highlands of eastern Kenya to the rain forests of Ivory Coast, has affected almost every African—and altered few governments."

WHEN TO USE THE COMMA
Use a comma if a quotation is introduced with or followed by an expression such as *she said* or *he uttered*.

> With a wry smile, <u>the firefighter remarked,</u> "Where there's smoke, there's fire."

> "I'm a Canadian," <u>I protested</u>.

WHEN A QUOTATION IS BLENDED INTO A SENTENCE
Use a comma or no punctuation depending on how the quotation fits into the grammatical structure of the sentence.

> She walked with an awkward jerky gait, as though she were not at home on her own legs, and as she passed by, the other kids would whisper, "Pigeon-Toed Cochran!"

> In summertime, all expeditions were planned tentatively; sentences ended with the phrase "if it doesn't rain."

WHEN A QUOTATION BEGINS A SENTENCE
Use a comma to set off a quotation at the beginning of a sentence.

> <u>"I'll be back in a moment,"</u> I told my students, and half out of my mind with anxiety, I went down in the lift, dashed across the street, and burst into Jai Lu's house.

However, a comma is not needed if the opening quotation ends with a question mark or an exclamation mark.

> "What are you doing?" I demanded.

WHEN A QUOTED SENTENCE IS INTERRUPTED BY EXPLANATORY WORDS
Use commas to set off the explanatory words.

> "No," <u>he called back</u>, "I can see it breathing!"

WHEN TWO SUCCESSIVE QUOTED SENTENCES ARE INTERRUPTED BY EXPLANATORY WORDS
Use a comma within the quotation marks of the first quotation. End the explanatory words with a period.

> "We are simply not well prepared for the rapid development that we have been experiencing," <u>Dr. Muangman said</u>. "Politicians and decision-makers think that if we make a lot of money, that is enough."

INCORRECT USES OF QUOTATION MARKS

Do not use quotation marks around indirect quotations.

> My mother always said longingly that she'd "like to visit Greece."

Do not use quotation marks to call attention to a word or expression. Never use quotation marks to distance yourself from an expression or to call attention to slang. Quotation marks used in this way are often called *scare quotes*. They are best avoided because they send an ambiguous message. Trust your words to speak for you, without the addition of quotation marks.

> Some might say the mechanic went on a "busman's holiday"

> Many academics find the language of "political correctness" objectionable.

Finally, do not use quotation marks to set off the title of your document.

Other Marks

PERIOD

Periods are commonly used to indicate the end of a sentence. They are also used in abbreviations.

ENDING SENTENCES
Use the period after statements, indirect questions, and mild commands.

STATEMENT
Use a period after a statement.

> Rock climbing on the Bruce Trail can be dangerous.

INDIRECT QUESTION
After a **direct question**, use a question mark.

> Do you want to walk the Gun Point Loop section of the trail?

However, if the question is **indirect**, use a period to end the sentence.

> The hike leader inquired if they wanted to walk the Gun Point Loop section of the trail.

MILD COMMAND
After a strong command, use the exclamation mark.

> Please, call an ambulance now!

However, after a **mild command**—an imperative or declarative sentence that is not an exclamation—use a period.

> Please pick up the groceries.

ABBREVIATIONS
Use periods in abbreviations such as the following:

> A.D. (or C.E.), a.m., B.A., B.C. (or B.C.E.), Dec., Dr., e.g., etc., i.e., Inc., Ltd., M.A., M.B.A., Mr., Mrs., Ms., p., p.m., Ph.D., St.

Do not use periods with Canada Post abbreviations, such as SK, ON, and NB.

Widely recognized abbreviations for organizations, companies, and countries do not require periods.

> CBC, CFL, CSIS, IBM, NBA, NFB UK, UN, USA

If you are in doubt about whether or not an abbreviation requires a period, check in a good Canadian dictionary or encyclopedia. To check the abbreviation of a name of a company, you might consult that company's website.

Do not add a second period if the sentence ends with an abbreviation's period.

> He always wanted to complete his M.A.

QUESTION MARK

FOLLOWING A DIRECT QUESTION
Use a question mark after any direct questions.

Are you coming or going?

Also use a question mark after a polite request.

Would you please forward me a copy of the article for my files?

Use a period after an indirect question.

Selby asked if she could go home.

FOLLOWING QUESTIONS IN A SERIES

Use a question mark to end each question in a series, even if series questions are not complete sentences.

We are curious to hear what Justin's career goal will be this week. Maybe a brain surgeon? A stock broker? Or perhaps a travel agent?

EXCLAMATION MARK

Use the exclamation mark with an emphatic declaration or a strong command.

The plane will hit the mountain!

Get out of the way, quickly!

Do not overuse the exclamation mark.

✗ We climbed the mountain on Hornby and had an incredible view! On one side was the snowcapped Coastal Range! On the other side, we could see majestic Mt. Washington!

✔ We climbed the mountain on Hornby and had an incredible view. On one side was the snowcapped Coastal Range. On the other side, we could see majestic Mt. Washington.

Communicate strong impressions through the powerful use of words, not through overuse of the exclamation mark.

DASH

The dash marks a strong break in the continuity of a sentence. It can be used to add information, to emphasize part of a sentence, or to set part of the sentence off for clarity.

To make a dash using your computer, enter two unspaced hyphens (--). Do not leave a space before the first hyphen or after the second hyphen. Many computer programs automatically format dashes when you enter two consecutive hyphens. This kind of dash is called an em dash (—). You can also select it in Word by going to the Insert menu, choosing Symbol and then selecting Em Dash from the Special Characters option or by pressing Ctrl, Alt, Minus on the numeric keyboard.

Dashes are used for the following purposes:

- to enclose a sentence element that interrupts the flow of thought, or to set off parenthetical material that deserves emphasis

> Our civilization is decadent and our language—so the argument runs—must inevitably share in the general collapse.
> —*George Orwell, "On Politics and Government"*
> *in* Shooting an Elephant and Other Essays
> *(London: Secker and Warburg, 1950).*

- to set off appositives that contain commas

> Teachers—those educators, parents, entertainers, babysitters, and counsellors—are undervalued and underpaid by society.

- to show a dramatic shift in tone or thought

> At the NBA All-Star Game, Michael Jordan took the pass, eluded the defender, hit full stride, soared—and missed an uncontested dunk.

- to restate

> Although they are close together—living only a few kilometres apart—they may as well be on different sides of the planet.

- to amplify

> Peanut butter was everywhere—in their hair, on their clothes, smudged on their glasses.

- to introduce a list

> In the storage room are all the paint supplies—paints, paint thinner, drop cloths, brushes, rollers, and paint trays.

Do not overuse dashes. If overused, dashes can lose their effectiveness and make writing disjointed. The Modern Language Association manual suggests limiting the number of dashes in a sentence to two paired dashes or one unpaired dash.

> ✗ Three students—Anwar, Sanjah, and Pete—won prizes—scholarships, books, and medallions. This is quite an achievement—especially for Pete, since he studies only minimally—if at all.

> ✔ Three students—Anwar, Sanjah, and Pete—won prizes, which included scholarships, books, and medallions. This is quite an achievement, especially for Pete, since he studies only minimally, if at all.

PARENTHESES

Parentheses are used to set off helpful, nonessential, additional information. While dashes usually call attention to the information they enclose, parentheses often de-emphasize the information they enclose.

Parentheses can be used for the following purposes:

- to enclose supplemental information, such as a definition, an example, a digression, an aside, or a contrast

  Calgary is second among cities in Canada for number of head offices located within its city limits (92 in 1995).

  Kenner taught at Assumption College (now University of Windsor) from 1946 to 1948.

- to enclose letters or numbers that label items in a series

  Follow these directions to make a puppet: (1) put your hand inside a white sock, (2) form the puppet's mouth with your thumb and fingers, and (3) draw a face on the sock with a felt-tipped marker.

Do not overuse parentheses. Including too much parenthetical information can make your writing seem choppy and awkward. Often, you can integrate information from parentheses into your sentences so they flow more smoothly.

The second phase of railway building in Canada ~~(starting 1867)~~ came with Confederation‸.in 1867

BRACKETS

Brackets (also called square brackets—not to be confused with parentheses) are used to enclose any words you have inserted into quoted material. You may need to add or change a word so a quotation will fit more smoothly into the structure of your sentences, or to clarify information or ideas for readers. As well, square brackets might be used to indicate an error in the original quoted material.

TO ADD OR SUBSTITUTE CLARIFYING INFORMATION IN A QUOTATION

"I rode swiftly toward Sitting Bull's camp. Then I saw the white soldiers [Reno's men] fighting in line."

The short passage is from *Bury My Heart at Wounded Knee* and offers oral accounts from a Native perspective of fighting between Native Americans and soldiers. The information in square brackets clarifies which white soldiers were doing the fighting.

TO INDICATE ERRORS IN ORIGINAL MATERIAL

The Latin word *sic* means "so" or "thus." The word *sic* is placed in square brackets immediately after a word in a quotation that appears erroneous or odd. *Sic* indicates that the word is quoted exactly as it stands in the original. The term is always in italics to indicate that it is a foreign word.

> "Growing up on the small island [*sic*] of Nanaimo, British Columbia, Diana Krall has made a name for herself as a jazz singer."

[Sic] indicates to the reader that the writer who is quoting the sentence realizes the author of the original article is wrong in calling Nanaimo an "island," when in fact it is a city.

ELLIPSIS MARK

An ellipsis mark consists of three spaced periods (. . .). The ellipsis is used to indicate that you have omitted material from the original writer's quoted words.

WHEN DELETING MATERIAL FROM A QUOTATION

> Gagnon states that "as much as 65% to 70% of semen volume originates from the seminal vesicles . . . and about 5% from the minor sexual glands."

An ellipsis is not required at the beginning of a quotation. Do not place an ellipsis at the end of the quotation, unless you have omitted content from the final quoted sentence.

WHEN DELETING A FULL SENTENCE FROM THE MIDDLE OF A QUOTED PASSAGE

Use a period before the three ellipsis points if you need to delete a full sentence or more from the middle of a quoted passage.

> Priestly's ideas on nationalism are not flattering. He says, "If we deduct from nationalism all that is borrowed or stolen from regionalism, what remains is mostly rubbish. . . . Almost all nationalist movements are led by ambitious, frustrated men determined to hold office."

WHEN QUOTING POETRY

Use a full line of spaced dots to indicate that you have omitted a line or more from the quotation of a poem.

Death, be not proud, though some have called thee
Mighty and dreadful, for thou art not so;
. . . .
From rest and sleep, which but thy pictures be,
Much pleasure; then from thee much more must flow,

—*John Donne*

WHEN INDICATING INTERRUPTION OR HESITATION IN SPEECH OR THOUGHT

Often in story dialogue or narration, an ellipsis is used to indicate hesitation or interruption in speech or thought.

"Well . . . I couldn't make it. I didn't get to the exam."

SLASH

USING THE SLASH TO INDICATE LINES OF POETRY

The slash is used most often in academic writing to mark off lines of poetry when these have been incorporated into the text. Up to three lines from a poem can be quoted in the text.

Atwood's "Death of a Young Son by Drowning" opens with the haunting lines, "He, who navigated with success / the dangerous river of his own birth / once more set forth."

Leave one space before and one space after the slash. For quoted passages of poetry that are four or more lines in length, start each line of the poem on its own line, indented in the style of block quotations.

USING THE SLASH TO INDICATE OPTIONS OR PAIRED ITEMS

Sometimes the slash is used between options or paired items. Examples include *actor/producer, life/death, pass/fail*. In these cases, do not leave a space before and after the slash.

Since the orchestra was short of funds, he served as artistic director/conductor.

Avoid the use of *he/she, his/her,* and *and/or,* as they are informal and awkward in writing.

MECHANICS
mechanics

"Proper names are rigid designators."

—SAUL KRIPKE

MECHANICS

Spelling and mechanics often make or break a document. Referring to "Robert Bondar" in a fundraising letter when you meant to refer to Canadian astronaut Roberta Bondar may have serious repercussions for your fundraising campaign and will certainly make the reader think twice about your credibility as a writer. Little things mean a lot.

Capitalization

Capitalize the first word of every sentence. You will also need to capitalize specific types of words within sentences. Use the following rules as general guidelines for capitalization. Consult your dictionary to determine which words must be capitalized.

PROPER VS. COMMON NOUNS

Capitalize proper nouns, and words derived from them, but do not capitalize common nouns. Proper nouns are the names of specific people, places, and things. Common nouns include all other nouns.

Usually, capitalize the following:

- names of religions, religious practitioners, holy books, special religious days, and deities
- geographic place names
- people's names and nicknames
- words of family relationship used as names (e.g., Uncle Bill)
- nationalities, tribes, races, and languages
- names of historical events, periods, movements, documents, and treaties
- political parties, organizations, and government departments
- educational institutions, departments, degrees, and specific courses
- names of celestial bodies
- names of ships, planes, and aircraft
- parts of letters (e.g., Dear John)
- names of specific software

Months, days of the week, and holidays are considered proper nouns. The seasons and numbers of days of the month are not considered proper nouns.

Every spring, <u>Victoria Day</u> falls on a <u>Monday</u> in <u>May</u>.

The meeting is held on the second <u>Tuesday</u> of <u>January</u>, <u>June</u>, and <u>December</u>.

CAPITALIZING NOUNS	
PROPER NOUNS	**COMMON NOUNS**
Zeus	a god
Book of Mormon	a book
Kamloops	a city
Marcel	a man
Aunt Agnes	my aunt
French	a language
Romanticism	a movement
New Democratic Party	a political party
Mars	a planet
the *Formidable*	a ship
Microsoft Word	a software program

Capitalize the names of school subjects only if they are languages, but capitalize the names of specific courses.

In his final year, he will need to take microbiology, chemistry, biology, <u>English</u>, and <u>Spanish</u>.

Professor Woodman teaches <u>Nineteenth-Century Literature</u> to all students majoring in English.

TITLES WITH PROPER NAMES

Capitalize the title of a person when it is part of a proper name.

<u>Dr.</u> Norman Bethune   <u>Rev.</u> David Rooke

<u>Professor</u> Gedalof   Douglas Fairbanks <u>Sr.</u>

<u>Judge</u> Shepperd gave his decision on the appeal.

Do not capitalize the title when it is used alone.

A <u>judge</u> presided over the inquiry.

Note: In some cases, if the title of an important public figure is used alone, the first letter can appear as either a capital letter or a lowercase letter. Conventions vary.

The <u>prime minister</u> [or <u>Prime Minister</u>] dodged the protester's pie.

TITLES OF WORKS

Capitalize the first, last, and all other important words in the titles of works such as books, articles, films, and songs.

IMPORTANT WORDS
These important words should be capitalized in titles and sub-titles:

- nouns
- verbs
- adjectives
- adverbs

LESS IMPORTANT WORDS
These less important words should not be capitalized *unless* they are the first or last word of the title or subtitle:

- articles
- prepositions
- coordinating conjunctions

Book Title: *A Feminist Dictionary*

Article Title: "A Turkey with Taste"

Film Title: *From Earth to the Moon*

Song Title: "Do You Know the Way to San José?"

Also use the guidelines above to capitalize chapter titles and other major divisions in a work.

"Phantom of the Canadian Opera: Trudeau's Revenge" is Chapter 11 in Peter C. Newman's *The Canadian Revolution*.

FIRST WORD OF A SENTENCE

Capitalize the first word of a sentence.

It's Monday morning, time for the weekly editorial meeting at a mass-market publishing house.

If a sentence appears within parentheses, capitalize the first word of the sentence. However, do not capitalize the first word if the parentheses are within another sentence.

The effects of plaque on the heart valves are significant. (See Figure 6.)

The effects of plaque on the heart valves are significant (see Figure 6).

FIRST WORD OF A QUOTED SENTENCE

Capitalize the first word of a direct quotation, but do not capitalize it if the quotation is blended into the sentence in which the quotation is introduced.

> The department chair defended the embattled professor, arguing, "He is an outstanding teacher, and the evidence against him is flimsy at best."

> In his article "Eco-tourism Boom: How Much Can Wildlife Take?" Bruce Obee says that "tour boats . . . are a fraction of the traffic."

If you need to interrupt a quoted sentence to include explanatory words, do not capitalize the first word following the interruption.

> "She goes by bus," the mother exclaimed with anger, "and I'm not very happy about that."

If you need to quote poetry in an essay, use the capitalization employed by the poet.

> Season of mists and mellow fruitfulness,
> Close bosom-friend of the maturing sun;
> Conspiring with him how to load and bless
> With fruit the vines that round the thatch-eves run; . . .
> —*John Keats, "To Autumn"*

Many modern poets do not follow the conventions of capitalization. When quoting their work, copy the text exactly.

> so much depends
> upon
> a red wheel
> barrow . . .
> —*William Carlos Williams, "The Red Wheelbarrow"*

FIRST WORD AFTER A COLON

When an independent clause appears after a colon, capitalizing the first word is optional; if the content after the colon is not an independent clause, do not capitalize.

> We were told to bring the following items for the hike: a compass, a sleeping bag, a tent, and enough food to last seven days.

There is one major reason that Phillip doesn't want Kathleen for a friend: he [*or* He] doesn't trust her.

ABBREVIATIONS

Capitalize the abbreviations for government departments and agencies, names of organizations and corporations, trade names, and call letters of television and radio stations.

> CSIS, CIA, NATO, CTV, *Loblaws Inc.*, CHCO-TV, CKNW

Abbreviations

In most cases, abbreviations should not be used in formal writing, such as academic essays, unless the abbreviations are very well known; for instance, *CBC* or *UN*. Abbreviations are more widely used in science and technical writing than in writing for the humanities.

Always consider your reader when deciding whether or not to use any abbreviation. Will he or she understand the abbreviation? One way to make sure is to use the full name at the first mention and include the abbreviation in parentheses immediately after it. From then on, the use of the abbreviation is acceptable. Otherwise, you run the risk of confusing the reader. If the type of writing that you are doing requires abbreviations, be consistent in your use of them.

TITLES WITH PROPER NAMES

Abbreviate titles and degrees immediately before and after proper names. Do not abbreviate a title or degree if it does not accompany a proper name.

> *professor*
> The ~~prof.~~ gave an inspiring lecture last Thursday.

Do not use titles and degrees redundantly:

> ✗ <u>Dr.</u> Steven Edwards, <u>M.D.</u>

> ✔ Dr. Steven Edwards

OR

> ✔ Steven Edwards, M.D.

ORGANIZATIONS, CORPORATIONS, AND COUNTRIES

Use standard abbreviations for names of countries, organizations, and corporations.

> UK (or U.K.), FBI, NORAD, RCMP, CIDA, TSN, RCA, IBM

To save money, she got a room at the YWCA.

If you need to use a less familiar abbreviation in your paper (e.g., COMECON, for the Council of Mutual Economic Assistance) do the following:

1. Write the full name of the organization, followed by the abbreviation in parentheses.
2. For each subsequent reference to the organization, use the abbreviation on its own.

B.C., A.D., A.M., P.M., NO.

Use the standard abbreviations B.C., A.D., *a.m.*, *p.m.*, and *no.* only with particular years, times, numbers, or amounts.

The abbreviation B.C. ("before Christ") or the acceptable alternative B.C.E. ("before the Common Era") always appears after a specific date.

156 B.C. (or B.C.E.)

The abbreviation A.D. (*Anno Domini*) appears before a specific date. C.E., an acceptable alternative meaning "Common Era," always appears after a specific date.

A.D. 65

65 C.E.

Use *a.m.*, *p.m.*, or *no.* only with a particular figure.

5:15 a.m. (or A.M.)

8:30 p.m. (or P.M.)

no. 16 (or No.)

In formal writing, do not use these abbreviations without particular figures.

We arrived for the dance in the early ~~p.m.~~ *afternoon.*

It is impossible to estimate the ~~no.~~ *number* of fish in the stream during spawning season.

LATIN ABBREVIATIONS

Since some readers may be unfamiliar with Latin abbreviations, keep use of these abbreviations to a minimum or use the English equivalent.

LATIN ABBREVIATIONS		
ABBREVIATION	LATIN	ENGLISH MEANING
c.	*circa*	approximately
cf.	*confer*	compare
e.g.	*exempli gratia*	for example
et al.	*et alii*	and others
etc.	*et cetera*	and the rest
i.e.	*id est*	that is
N.B.	*nota bene*	note well
P.S.	*postscriptum*	postscript
vs.	*versus*	versus

In informal writing, such as personal e-mails, it is acceptable to use Latin abbreviations.

Jennifer wants to go the Raptors game this Tuesday. It's the Raptors vs. the Sonics. After the game let's grab a burger, etc. N.B. Dominique and her gang will be there.

In formal writing, use the full English words or phrases.

The Sumerians came down to the bank of the Euphrates and Tigris rivers ~~c.~~ *around* 3500 B.C.E. Many artifacts—~~e.g.,~~ *for example* the headdress of Queen Sub-ad and the bronze mask portrait of King Sargon—provide evidence of their cultural advancement.

MISUSES

Abbreviations are generally not appropriate in formal writing.

Margaret Atwood is a popular author in ~~Can. lit.~~ classes *(Canadian literature)* because she has written so many outstanding novels.

TYPES OF ABBREVIATION TO AVOID IN FORMAL WRITING		
CATEGORY	FORMAL	INFORMAL
Names of Persons	Jennifer	Jen
Holidays	Christmas	Xmas
Days of the Week	Tuesday to Thursday	Tues. to Thurs.
Months	from January to August	from Jan. to Aug.
Provinces and Countries	Saskatchewan	Sask. or SK
Academic Subjects	Biology and English	Bio. and Engl.
Units of Measurement*	6 ounces	6 oz.
Addresses	Madison Avenue	Madison Ave.
Subdivision of Books	chapter, page	ch., p.**

*except metric measurements
**except as part of documentation

Metric abbreviations are often permitted in formal writing, as in 25 *kg* or 15 *mm*. However, do not use a number written in words with an abbreviation, as in *twenty cm*.

Abbreviations are acceptable in company or institution names only if the abbreviation is part the company's or institution's official name, as in *Jack's Windows & Roofing Co.,* or *Writers Inc. Consulting*. Never arbitrarily abbreviate a company's name. For example, if a company's name is *Randolph Architectural Group*, do not shorten it to *Randolph Arch. Gr.* When corresponding with any company, use the full company name that appears on company stationery or in the firm's advertising, or on its website.

Spelling

Checking spelling should be one of the final steps in your writing process, and it is an extremely important step.

Spell checkers in word-processing programs can be useful tools for helping you spot some potential spelling problems. However, spell checkers have limitations that allow many spelling errors to be missed. These limitations include the following:

- Many spell checkers, in their default setting, do not include Canadian spellings. It is, however, often possible to select Canadian spelling. As well, dictionaries such as *The Canadian Oxford Dictionary* are available in CD-ROM and can be installed and used to do the spell checking.
- Countless words, such as new or marginal words or very specialized vocabularies, are not included. For instance, if you type *tchotchkes* (meaning "cheap, showy trinkets"), the spell checker may offer you "crotches" as a correction—not what you had in mind at all.
- Spell checkers cannot distinguish between commonly confused words that have entirely different meanings (e.g., *allusion* and *illusion*).
- They cannot intuit that you have made a simple typographical error, such as using *do* when you meant *to*.
- The majority of proper nouns are not included.

Rumour has it that, in one early spell checker, a common misspelling of *inconvenience* ("inconvinence") was corrected to read *incontinence*; well-meaning people who didn't proofread carefully ended up with *Sorry for the incontinence* instead of *Sorry for the inconvenience*. Mistakes of this kind could prove very embarrassing, to say the least.

Spell checkers tend to make writers dependent. This leads to some automaticity. To avoid overreliance on spell checkers, bear in mind that your spell checker needs to reflect Canadian spelling, and that it needs to be supplemented by proofreading, to catch spelling errors caused by words that sound alike, which cannot be caught by computerized means.

BRITISH AND U.S. VARIATIONS

In your reading, you might notice variations in spellings for certain words. For instance, if you are reading an American article, you might encounter *traveled*, while in a Canadian article you would see *travelled*. Similarly, in a British article you might find *apologise*, while a Canadian article would use *apologize*. Consistently use Canadian spellings in your writing. Generally, Canadian spelling follows British usage in its treatment of *-our* words (*colour* not *color*) and *-re* words (*centre* not *center*), as well as doubling certain consonants before a suffix beginning with a vowel (*counsellor* not *counselor*), but follows American style for *-ize* words (*organize* not *organise*). Check the preferred spelling in a good Canadian dictionary, where the Canadian spelling will be listed first.

WORDS THAT SOUND ALIKE

Words that sound the same but have different meanings and spellings are called **homophones**. Homophones are often the source of spelling problems. As you proofread your work, look carefully for homophones you may have used or spelled incorrectly.

COMMONLY CONFUSED WORDS

accept	*a verb meaning "to receive"*
except	*a preposition meaning "other" or verb meaning "to exclude"*
affect	*a verb meaning "to cause change"*
effect	*usually a noun meaning "the result of change"*
cite	*a verb meaning "to quote"*
site	*a noun meaning "location"*
sight	*a noun meaning "vision"*
desert	*a verb meaning "to abandon"*
dessert	*a noun meaning "sweet course after the main course of a meal"*
its	*a possessive pronoun meaning "belonging to it"*
it's	*a contraction of it is*
loose	*an adjective meaning "not well attached"*
lose	*a verb meaning "to misplace" or "to part with"*
principal	*a noun meaning "the chief person" (as in a school), or adjective meaning "main"*
principle	*a noun meaning "a basic truth"*
their	*a possessive pronoun meaning "belonging to them"*
they're	*a contraction of they are*
there	*an adverb meaning "in that place"*

who's	*a contraction of* who is *or* who has
whose	*the possessive form of* who
your	*the possessive form of* you
you're	*a contraction of* you are

The Glossary of Usage contains many homophones, as well as words that sound nearly the same and can cause spelling problems. There you will also find definitions for each word in the following sets of words.

HOMOPHONES AND SIMILAR-SOUNDING SETS OF WORDS IN THE GLOSSARY OF USAGE

accept, except	*elicit, illicit*
adapt, adopt	*emigrate, immigrate*
adverse, averse	*eminent, imminent*
advice, advise	*everyone, every one*
affect, effect	*explicit, implicit*
aggravate, irritate	*farther, further*
all ready, already	*ingenious, ingenuous*
all together, altogether	*its, it's*
allude, elude	*lead, led*
allusion, illusion	*licence, license*
amoral, immoral	*loose, lose*
anyone, any one	*maybe, may be*
awhile, a while	*moral, morale*
beside, besides	*passed, past*
capital, capitol	*practice, practise*
censor, censure	*precede, proceed*
cite, site	*principal, principle*
climactic, climatic	*respectfully, respectively*
coarse, course	*sometime, some time, sometimes*
complement, compliment	*stationary, stationery*
conscience, conscious	*than, then*
continual, continuous	*there, their, they're to, too, two*
council, counsel	*weather, whether*
discreet, discrete	*who's, whose*
disinterested, uninterested	*your, you're*

Checking writing drafts for spelling errors demands your complete attention, and a computer spell checker is just one of many tools and strategies at your disposal.

Once you have mastered these spelling strategies, there are three more you can apply to help ensure that any manuscript you submit is free of spelling errors.

1. Proofread drafts meticulously to identify and fix any spelling problems.
2. Keep a dictionary nearby to check the spelling of words you do not know; have access to specialized dictionaries or other resources to check concerns you have about spelling specialized vocabulary.
3. Make and maintain a list of your own recurrent spelling problems; focus on list items as you proofread your draft so you don't repeat these errors.

DOCUMENTATION
documentation

MLA STYLE OF DOCUMENTATION

Writers in the arts and humanities generally follow the Modern Language Association (MLA) guidelines for formatting research papers and documenting sources. This chapter summarizes MLA style guidelines published in the *MLA Handbook for Writers of Research Papers*, 7th ed. (New York: MLA, 2009) and concludes with some pages from a model research paper following MLA format and documentation style.

If a reader, such as your instructor, wants to check any source you used for words, facts, or ideas, he or she needs complete information about your sources. When following MLA style, you document your sources in two ways:

1. Within the body of the paper, using **in-text citations**
2. At the end of the paper, in a list of **works cited**

In-Text Citations

An in-text citation consists of a **parenthetical reference** that gives the minimum information necessary to identify a source and locate the relevant material within it. Most often, this is the author's last name (unless the signal phrase mentions the author's name) and a page number or numbers. Full information on the source is supplied in the list of works cited.

IN-TEXT REFERENCES TO AUTHORS

AUTHOR MENTIONED IN A SIGNAL PHRASE
A signal phrase indicates that something taken from a source—for example, a quotation, summary, or paraphrase—is about to be used. When you mention the author's name in a signal phrase, give only the page reference within the parentheses. Note that the parentheses are inside the end punctuation.

> Peter Schrag observes that America is "divided between affluence and poverty, between slums and suburbs" (118).

AUTHOR NOT MENTIONED IN A SIGNAL PHRASE
If the author's name is not mentioned in a signal phrase, it must appear in parentheses along with the page reference. No punctuation is required between the author's name and the page reference.

> One commentator notes that America is "divided between affluence and poverty, between slums and suburbs" (Schrag 118).

TWO OR MORE WORKS BY THE SAME AUTHOR

When you use two or more works by the same author in a research paper, you will have multiple entries for that author in your list of works cited. Your in-text citation must direct the reader to the correct entry. You can do this in one of three ways:

1. If you have provided the author's name and the title of the work in the signal phrase, include only the page number(s) in parentheses.

   In *Lament for a Nation*, George Grant claims that "modern civilization makes all local cultures anachronistic" (54).

2. If only the author's name is given in the signal phrase, include the title of the work (abbreviated if the title is long) within the parenthetical reference.

   George Grant claims that "modern civilization makes all local cultures anachronistic" (*Lament* 54).

3. If there is no signal phrase, the parenthetical reference should include the author's last name, the title or a shortened version of it, and the page number(s). Use a comma to separate the author's name and the title.

   Some propose that "modern civilization makes all local cultures anachronistic" (Grant, *Lament* 54).

TWO OR THREE AUTHORS

You can include the names of the authors in the signal phrase or place them within the parenthetical reference.

   According to Clarkson and McCall, even late in the decade of the Quiet Revolution, "Trudeau saw the constitutional question as only one facet of his general mandate for the Justice Department" (258).

   Even late in the decade of the Quiet Revolution, "Trudeau saw the constitutional question as only one facet of his general mandate for the Justice Department" (Clarkson and McCall 258).

   With three authors, use a serial comma in the reference:

   (Wynkin, Blynkin, and Nodd viii)

MORE THAN THREE AUTHORS

If the work you are citing has more than three authors, you have two options:

1. Name only the first author and use *et al.* (Latin abbreviation for "and others").
2. Give all names in full.

The method you choose should match the one you use in the list of works cited.

> One position is that "in cultures whose religion, unlike Christianity, offers no promise of an afterlife, a name that will live on after one's death serves as the closest substitute for immortality" (Abrams et al. 3).

Note that *al.* takes a period (it is an abbreviation), but *et* does not.

CORPORATE AUTHOR

A corporate author is a company, an agency, or an institution that is credited with authorship of a work and is treated like an individual author. Since long references tend to be disruptive, put long names in a signal phrase if possible. For long names in parentheses, shorten terms that are commonly abbreviated.

> The former Council of Biology Editors states in the previous edition of the style manual that "any coordinate system must be based upon a known reference point" (241).

> The previous edition of the style manual states that "any coordinate system must be based upon a known reference point" (Council 241).

NO AUTHOR

If there is no author named, the parenthetical citation should give the full title (if brief) or a shortened version, unless the title appears in a signal phrase. The following example illustrates a reference to a magazine article, with the shortened title enclosed in quotation marks.

> The incidence of deep vein thrombosis, the so-called Economy Class Syndrome, has been associated with a genetic predisposition to this type of blood clotting ("Flying" 8).

IN-TEXT REFERENCES TO PRINT SOURCES

MULTIVOLUME WORK

If you cite specific material from a multivolume work, in the parenthetical reference include the volume number followed by a colon, a space, and then the page reference. Do not include the words *volume* or *page* or their abbreviations.

> Abram et al. state that "the period of more than four hundred years that followed the Norman Conquest presents a much more diversified picture than the Old English period" (1: 5).

If you are referring to an entire volume of a multivolume work, however, it is not necessary to cite the page(s). The author's name is followed by a comma and the abbreviation *vol.* (Abram et al., vol. 1). Note that if such a reference is included in a signal phrase, *volume* should be spelled out.

LITERARY WORK
Since literary works are often available in different editions and therefore have different page numbering, you should refer to a particular chapter, act, scene, or line, using appropriate abbreviations.

NOVEL
When citing a passage from a novel, the parenthetical reference should give the page number followed by a semicolon and other identifying information.

> In Atwood's *The Robber Bride*, Tony reveals a distorted picture of Zenia: "She has thought of Zenia as tearless, more tearless even than herself. And now there are not only tears but many tears, rolling fluently down Zenia's strangely immobile face, which always looks made-up even when it isn't" (190; ch. 25).

POETRY
When citing lines from poems and verse plays, omit page numbers and cite the division (e.g., act, scene, book, or part) and then the line, using periods (without spaces) to separate the numbers.

> In *Civil Elegies*, Lee describes Canadians' relationship with the rugged land:
>
>> We live on occupied soil.
>> Across the barren Shield, immortal scrubland and our own,
>> where near the beginning the spasms of lava settled to bedrock schist,
>> barbaric land, initial, our own, scoured bare under
>> crush of the glacial recessions (3.40–46)

DRAMA
Include the act, scene, and line numbers in the parenthetical citation. Use Arabic numerals unless instructed otherwise.

> Shakespeare establishes the dark mood of *Macbeth* in the second witch's response to the *first* witch's query on when they should meet again: "When the battle's lost and won" (1.1.3).

The Bible

When citing a passage from the Bible, include—either in the signal phrase or the parenthetical reference—the book, chapter, and verse. Books of the Bible may be abbreviated in a parenthetical reference if you wish (e.g., 1 Chron. 13.4, Rev. 20.2).

Work in an Anthology

If you are referencing a particular part of an anthology—for example, an essay or a story—name the author of that piece rather than the editor of the anthology. The list of works cited gives additional information about the anthology and the editor.

INDIRECT SOURCE

Although you should try to use original sources, if your only option is an indirect source, begin the citation in the parenthetical reference with the abbreviation *qtd. in* ("quoted in").

> To Woody Allen, the successful monologue is a matter of attitude: "I can only surmise that you have to give the material a fair shake at the time and you have to deliver it with confidence" (qtd. in Lax 134).

ENTIRE WORK

When citing an entire work, it is preferable to provide the author's name in a signal phrase rather than a parenthetical reference. No page reference is required. The corresponding entry in the list of works cited provides publication information. This also applies to works with no page numbers, such as a film or television program.

> In *The Second Sex*, Simone de Beauvoir brilliantly argues her position on women's inequality.

MORE THAN ONE WORK IN A SINGLE CITATION

Cite each work as you normally would, using semicolons to separate the citations.

> An understanding of the business cycle is fundamental to successful investing (Gardner 69; Lasch 125).

ELECTRONIC SOURCES

The MLA guidelines for in-text citations of electronic sources are the same as those for print sources. However, many online sources do not include a page numbering system. You should not take page numbers from a printout, as pagination may vary in different printouts. Some electronic sources use alternative systems, numbering text by paragraph, section, or screen, but others do not. Here are some guidelines for situations you may encounter when citing electronic sources.

THE ELECTRONIC SOURCE HAS AN AUTHOR AND FIXED PAGE NUMBERS
Give both the author's name and the page numbers, with the author's name either in the signal phrase or the parenthetical reference.

> According to Caroline Spurgeon, "The main image in *Othello* is that of animals in action, preying upon one another, mischievous, lascivious, cruel or suffering, and throughout the general sense of pain and unpleasantness is much increased and kept constantly before us" (2).

THE ELECTRONIC SOURCE HAS AN AUTHOR BUT NO PAGE NUMBER
If the electronic source uses an alternative numbering system, use it to cite a specific location in the source, abbreviating "paragraph(s)" as *par.* or *pars.* and "section" as *sec.*

> Fackrell asserts the accommodation for animals is adequate: "We have lodgings for up to 12 dogs at a time in our indoor/outdoor runs" (par. 9).

THE ELECTRONIC SOURCE HAS NO NUMBERING SYSTEM
Give the author's name where possible and cite the entire work in the list of works cited.

> Human rights violations are said to be decreasing as a result of foreign aid initiatives in the region (Danko).

THE ELECTRONIC SOURCE HAS NO AUTHOR
If the author of the electronic source is not known, either use the complete title in the signal phrase or use a shortened form of the title in the parenthetical reference.

> According to a webpage sponsored by Children Now, an American organization that provides support for children and families, "52% of girls and 53% of boys say there are enough good role models for girls in television, although more girls (44%) than boys (36%) say there are too few" (*Reflections of Girls*).

List of Works Cited

When you are following the MLA documentation style—a list of works cited—compile the list on a separate page at the end of your paper. The list provides essential publication information for each of the sources cited in your paper and simplifies documentation by allowing you to make only brief references to these works in the text. Include in your list of works cited only the sources from which you quoted, paraphrased, or summarized information. Do not include sources that you consulted but did not refer to in your paper. (Some instructors may require an additional listing of works consulted.)

FORMAT OF A LIST OF WORKS CITED

TITLE AND PLACEMENT

Start the list of works cited on a new page at the end of your research paper. Title it *Works Cited* and centre the title at the top of the page. The title *Works Cited* allows you to include books and articles, as well as films, recordings, websites, television programs, and other non-print sources.

PAGINATION

Continue the page numbering of the text throughout the list of works cited; for example, if the last page of your research paper is 15, the first page of *Works Cited* would be 16. Position page numbers in the upper right-hand corner.

SPACING

Double-space within and between entries.

INDENTATION

Begin each entry at the left margin; if an entry runs more than one line, indent the subsequent line or lines 1.25 cm (0.5 in.) from the left margin.

ARRANGEMENT OF ENTRIES

Alphabetize entries in the list of works cited by the last name of the author. For entries with more than one author that begin with the same author name, alphabetize according to the last names of the second authors listed. If a source has no author or editor, alphabetize by the title, ignoring any initial articles (*A, An,* or *The*).

For a sample list of works cited, refer to the model essay provided at the end of this chapter.

Examples of Works Cited entries are shown below. If you encounter sources that are not covered here, consult the *MLA Handbook for Writers of Research Papers*, 7th ed. (New York: MLA, 2009).

BOOKS

There are four main units of information in a book entry. They are (1) author's name, (2) book title, (3) publication information, and (4) medium.

Author's name   Book title

Seabrook, John. *Nobrow: The Culture of Marketing—The*

Marketing of Culture. New York: Knopf, 2000. Print.

                       Publication information   Medium

The publication details for a book are found on the **title page** and on the reverse side of the title page, which is known as the **copyright page**. A very few books have publication information at the back of the book. When writing an entry, use information from the source itself as opposed to information from a bibliography or library catalogue. This will reduce the chance of errors in your entry.

AUTHOR'S NAME
Place the last name first, followed by a comma and a space, and then the first name and initials, if any are included on the title page. Leave a space between two initials. Put a period after the complete name.

BOOK TITLE
Provide the full name of the book, including any subtitles. The entire title, but not the period following it, should be italicized. Capitalize important words within the title. If there is a subtitle, separate it from the main title with a colon and one space. Always capitalize the first and last words in any subtitle. End the title with a period and leave one space before the publication information.

TITLE WITHIN A TITLE
- If a title within an underlined title would normally be italicized, neither italicize it nor place it in quotation marks.

  White, E. B. *Writings from* The New Yorker *1927–1976.* Ed.

      Rebecca M. Dale. New York: HarperPerennial, 1991. Print.

- If a title within an italicized title would normally be in quotation marks, keep them. Note that the period is inside the quotation marks.

  Card, James Van Dyck. *An Anatomy of "Penelope."*

      Rutherford: Farleigh Dickinson UP, 1984. Print.

- For a title within a title in quotation marks, italicize it if that is what you would normally do. If you would normally use quotation marks, use single quotation marks.

Publication Information

PLACE OF PUBLICATION: If several cities are listed on the title or copyright pages, use only the first. Place a colon and one space between the place of publication and the name of the publisher. For cities outside the United States that may be unfamiliar or ambiguous, add a comma and the province or country in abbreviated form. For example, if London, Ontario, is meant rather than London, England, write *London, ON*. For a foreign city, you may substitute the English name or add a translation in brackets.

PUBLISHER: You do not need to use the complete name of the publisher; simply give enough information to enable your reader to find the source easily. Omit any articles (*A, An, The*), common abbreviations (*Inc., Co.,* and *Ltd.*), and descriptive words (*Books, House, Press,* and *Publishers*). However, for university presses, always include the abbreviations *U* and *P* or *UP* as the case may be (e.g., *Oxford UP* or *U of Chicago P*) because the university itself may publish independently of its press. If the publishing company includes the name of one person, cite the surname alone (*Norton* rather than *W. W. Norton*). If it includes two names, cite the first surname only (*McGraw* rather than *McGraw-Hill*). Place a comma between the name of the publisher and the year of publication.

YEAR OF PUBLICATION: If no date appears on the title page, use the latest copyright date.

SINGLE AUTHOR

Cameron, Julia. *The Sound of Paper: Starting from Scratch.*

New York: Penguin, 2004. Print.

TWO OR THREE AUTHORS

Give the authors' names in the same order as they appear on the title page, which may not be in alphabetical order. Reverse the name of the first author only, add a comma, and give the other name(s) in normal order. Use *and* rather than an ampersand (&) before the last name in the list. Place a period after the last name.

McKercher, Catherine, and Carman Cumming. *The Canadian*

Reporter: News Writing and Reporting. Toronto:

Harcourt, 1998. Print.

Petty, Walter T., Dorothy C. Petty, and Marjorie F. Becking.

Experiences in Language: Tools and Techniques for

Language Arts Methods. Boston: Allyn 1973. Print.

MORE THAN THREE AUTHORS

Gini-Newman, Garfield, Bob Aitken, Diane Eaton, Dick

Holland, John Montgomery, and Sonia Riddock.

Ontario Edition: Canada: A Nation Unfolding. Toronto:

McGraw, 2000. Print.

EDITOR(S)

Richler, Mordecai, ed. *The Best of Modern Humour.* Toronto:

McClelland, 1983. Print.

EDITION (AUTHOR WITH AN EDITOR)

Brontë, Charlotte. *Jane Eyre.* Ed. Susan Cockcroft. Cambridge:

Cambridge UP, 1996. Print.

TRANSLATION

Apuleius. *The Golden Ass.* Trans. Jack Lindsay. Bloomington:

Indiana UP, 1962. Print.

CORPORATE AUTHOR

PriceWaterhouseCoopers. *Technology Forecast: 2000.* Menlo

Park: PriceWaterhouseCoopers Technology Center,

2000. Print.

ANONYMOUS WORK

Begin the entry with the title, ignoring any initial article (*A, An, The*). In the example below, the word *Second* would be used to alphabetize the entry.

"The Second Shepherds' Pageant." *Everyman and Medieval*

Miracle Plays. Ed. A. C. Cawley. New York: Dutton,

1959. Print.

TWO OR MORE WORKS BY THE SAME AUTHOR

Give the name of the author in the first entry only. In succeeding entries, type three hyphens followed by a period in place of the author's name. Then provide the title and publication information. Alphabetize by title.

Roth, Philip. *The Human Stain*. Boston: Houghton, 2000. Print.

---. *Patrimony: A True Story*. New York: Simon, 1991. Print.

If an author is the coauthor of a second entry, do not use three hyphens; begin the second entry with the author's full name.

SECOND OR SUBSEQUENT EDITION

Strunk, William, Jr., and E. B. White. *The Elements of Style*.

3rd ed. New York: Macmillan, 1979. Print.

MULTIVOLUME WORK

Cite the number of volumes after the title (and editor or edition, if any) and before the publication information, using the abbreviation *vols*. Do not indicate any specific volume or page number(s) here; rather, supply these in the parenthetical reference in the text.

Daymond, Douglas, and Leslie Monkman, eds. *Literature in*

Canada. 2 vols. Toronto: Gage, 1978. Print.

If you used only one of the volumes, give the volume number and publication information for that volume alone. In this case, give only page numbers in the parenthetical citation. You may add the total number of volumes at the end of the entry.

Daymond, Douglas, and Leslie Monkman, eds. *Literature in*

Canada. Vol. 2. Toronto: Gage, 1978. 2 vols. Print.

ENCYCLOPEDIA, DICTIONARY, OR OTHER REFERENCE WORK

If the articles in the source are arranged alphabetically, you do not need to provide the volume and page numbers. If the reference is familiar, you may also omit publication information. These sources may be listed in a shortened form as follows:

1. Author of the article (if known)
2. Title of the article, in quotation marks
3. Title of the source, italicized
4. Edition (if stated)
5. Year of publication
6. Medium

Boles, Glen. "Mount Assiniboine." *The Canadian*

Encyclopedia. 2000 ed. 1999. Print.

WORK IN AN ANTHOLOGY

Fitzgerald, Penelope. "At Hiruharama." *New Writing*. Ed.

Malcolm Bradbury and Judy Cooke. London: Minerva,

1992. 33–39. Print.

For two or more works published in a single anthology, you may create a complete entry for the anthology and cross-reference individual pieces to the entry.

1. Create a complete entry for the anthology.

Remnick, David, and Henry Finder, eds. *Fierce Pajamas: An*

Anthology of Humor Writing from The New Yorker.

New York: Random, 2001. Print.

2. Create a separate entry for each piece in the anthology, giving the author and title. Then cross-reference to the anthology by giving the last name(s) of the anthology editor(s) and the inclusive page numbers for the piece. The following are examples of cross-references to the anthology entry shown above.

Brickman, Marshall. "The Analytic Napkin." Remnick and

Finder 25–28. Print.

Geng, Veronica. "My Mao." Remnick and Finder 95–99. Print.

INTRODUCTION, PREFACE, FOREWORD, OR AFTERWORD

Green, Richard. Introduction. *The Consolation of Philosophy*.

By Boethius. Trans. Richard Green. Indianapolis: Bobbs-

Merrill, 1962. ix–xxiii. Print.

BOOK IN A SERIES

Give the author name(s) and the title of the work, followed by a period and the publication information. The series name appears at the end of the listing. It is not underlined or enclosed in quotation marks and is commonly abbreviated.

Lecker, Robert, Jack David, and Ellen Quigley. *Bissoondath,*

Clarke, Kogawa, Mistry, Skvorecky. Toronto: ECW, 1996.

Print. Can. Writers and Their Works 11.

REPUBLISHED BOOK

Place the original publication date after the title and then give the republishing information. When the republication includes new material, such as an afterword, include the information after the original publication date.

Moodie, Susanna. *Roughing It in the Bush*. 1852. Afterword

Susan Glickman. Toronto: McClelland, 1989. Print.

ARTICLES

ARTICLE IN A MONTHLY MAGAZINE

Give the author name followed by a period, the name of the article in quotation marks with a period inside. Follow with the name of the magazine, italicized, the month and year of publication, and then a colon and a space. Then provide the medium. With the exception of May, June, and July, abbreviate the months. Volume and issue number should not be included. Last, give the inclusive page numbers for the entire article, followed by a period. If the article is not printed on consecutive pages, give only the first page number and a plus sign (+).

Bass, George F. "Golden Age Treasures." *National Geographic*

Mar. 2002: 102–17. Print.

ARTICLE IN A WEEKLY MAGAZINE
Follow the same general pattern as for a monthly magazine, but add the day of publication before the month.

> Begley, Sharon. "The Schizophrenic Mind." *Newsweek* 11 Mar.
>
> 2002: 44–51. Print.

ARTICLE IN A JOURNAL PAGINATED BY VOLUME
Some journals use continuous pagination, with all issues published in a single year collected in one volume. The pages in these volumes are usually numbered in continuous sequence, with the numbering beginning at 1 in the next volume. However, include the issue number whenever it is available. To cite an article in a volume with continuous pagination, give the journal title, volume number, issue number, year of publication in parentheses, followed by a colon, a space, inclusive page numbers, a period, and then the medium.

> Strain, Laurel A. "Seniors' Centres: Who Cares?" *Canadian*
>
> *Journal of Aging* 20.4 (2001): 471–91. Print.

ARTICLE IN A JOURNAL PAGINATED ONLY BY ISSUE
If the journal uses only issue numbers, you must give the issue number to locate the source. Give the issue number alone, followed by a period and no space, the year, inclusive page numbers, a period, and the medium.

> Frickle, Michele. "In This Pure Land." *Surface Design Journal*
>
> 25. (2002): 26–29. Print.

ARTICLE IN A DAILY NEWSPAPER

> Conlogue, Ray. "All the News of 1752." *Globe and Mail* 4 Mar.
>
> 2002: R1+. Print.

ANONYMOUS ARTICLE

> "Northern Rockies Whopper." *Beautiful British Columbia*
>
> Spring 1998: 46. Print.

EDITORIAL
Add the word *Editorial* after the title, followed by a period. For unsigned editorials, begin with the title.

"Where Justice Stumbled." Editorial. *Globe and Mail* 4 Mar.

2001: A10. Print.

LETTER TO THE EDITOR

Kennedy, Paul. Letter. *Harper's* Sept. 2002: 4. Print.

REVIEW

Gartner, Zsuzsi. "In Search of a Vanished Zeitgeist." Rev. of

The Doctor's House, by Ann Beattie. *Globe and Mail* 2

Mar. 2002: D3. Print.

For a film review, instead of *by* use *dir.* (for *director* or *directed by*).

Ansen, David. "Brave Heart of Darkness." Rev. of *We Were*

Soldiers, dir. Randall Wallace. *Newsweek* 11 Mar. 2002:

63. Print.

For a review of a performance such as theatre, dance, or music, add any significant details about the production.

Walker, Susan. "Spanish Dance Troupe Goes Wild in the

Garden." Rev. of Senza Tempo dance/theatre troupe.

Power of Place. Harbourfront Centre, Toronto. *Toronto*

Star 29 June 2006: G6. Print.

ELECTRONIC SOURCES

Citations for electronic sources serve the same purposes as do citations for print sources, and there are similarities in their formats. However, because standards for electronic media are less well established, a reader requires optimal information to locate many electronic sources.

Bear in mind that documentation styles for electronic sources are still evolving and updates are sometimes posted online. For articles on documenting electronic sources, visit the Frequently Asked Questions page at the MLA website, www.mla.org/style_faq.

The list below indicates the information to include in a Works Cited entry for an online source. No source will require all items on the list. Choose those that are relevant and available, following the order shown below.

1. *Author*: Name of the author (or editor, compiler, or translator), last name first, using appropriate abbreviations (e.g., *ed.*).
2. *Title A*: Title of a poem, short story, article, or similar short work, placed in quotation marks and followed by a period. If the source is a posting to a discussion list or forum, take the title from the subject line and follow it with *Online posting* (not in italics) and a period.
3. *Title B*: Title of a book, italicized.
4. *Editor*: Name(s) of the editor, compiler, or translator if cited earlier. The name is not inverted, and it is preceded by *Ed.*, *Comp.*, or *Trans.*
5. *Print version*: Publication details about any print version of the source, including date of original print publication.
6. *Title C*: Title of the Internet site, italicized; if there is no title, a description such as *Home page*, not italicized.
7. *Site editor*: Name(s) of the editor or director of the scholarly project or database, if given, preceded by *Ed.*, *Eds.*, or *Dir.*
8. *Version*: Version number, if not part of the title; for a journal, the volume number, issue number, or other identifying number.
9. *Date 1*: Date of electronic publication, update, or posting.
10. *Subscription service*: Name of the service, and, if a library is the subscriber, the library name and city (and province or state abbreviation, if needed), separated by commas.
11. *List or forum*: Name of the discussion list or forum, if applicable.
12. *Pages*: Number range (e.g., 16–27) or total number of pages (*pp.*), paragraphs (*pars.*), or other sections (*secs.*), if they are numbered.
13. *Sponsor*: Name of any institution or organization sponsoring or associated with the website.
14. *Medium*: Web.
15. *Date 2*: Date when you accessed the source.
16. *URL*: Because of their ever-changing nature, complete electronic addresses of the source are no longer required in MLA style. If you do decide to include the URL, you may do so (in angle brackets); or, for a subscription service, the URL of the service's home page (if known) or the name assigned by the service, preceded by keyword. Include the access-mode identifier (*http, flp, gopher, telnet, news*) and any relevant path and file names. If a URL runs over a line, break it only after a slash and ensure no hyphens are inadvertently added at line breaks. A final period appears after the closing angle bracket containing the URL.

SOURCE IN SCHOLARLY PROJECT OR REFERENCE DATABASE

"Charles George Douglas Roberts." The Electronic Text

Centre. Dir. Alan Burk. 1996. U of New Brunswick

Libraries. Web. 5 Mar. 2002.

Frost, Robert. "Mowing." *A Boy's Will*. New York: Henry Holt,

1915. *Project Bartleby Archive*. Ed. Steven van

Leeuwen. Dec. 1995. Columbia U. Web. 6 Mar. 2002

<http://www.bartleby.com/117/19.html>.

ENTIRE ONLINE SCHOLARLY PROJECT

The Complete Writings and Pictures of Dante Gabriel Rossetti:

A Hypermedia Archive. Ed. Jerome McCann. 1993–

2008. Institute for Advanced Technology in the

Humanities, U of Virginia. Web. 2 Nov. 2011.

PERSONAL WEBSITE

Rockwell, Geoffrey. Home page. 2004. Web. 2 Nov. 2011

<http://www.geoffreyrockwell.com>.

PROFESSIONAL WEBSITE

Epic Records. 2001. Sony Music Inc. Web. 18 Mar. 2006.

ONLINE BOOK

Keats, John. *Poetical Works*. London, 1884. *Bartleby.com:*

Great Books Online. Ed. Steven van Leeuwen. 2002.

Web. 4 July 2006.

ONLINE BOOK IN SCHOLARLY PROJECT OR REFERENCE DATABASE

Dickens, Charles. *A Tale of Two Cities*. 1859. Literature.org.

Ed. Peter Galbavy. 23 May 2005. Web. 3 July 2006.

ARTICLE IN ONLINE SCHOLARLY JOURNAL

Rist, Thomas. "Religion, Politics, Revenge: The Dead in

Renaissance Drama." *Early Modern Literary Studies* 9.1

(2003): 20 pars. Web. 3 July 2006.

ARTICLE IN ONLINE MAGAZINE

Nyhan, Brendan. "Bully Brigade." *Salon.com*. 5 Mar. 2002.

Web. 4 July 2006.

ARTICLE IN ONLINE NEWSPAPER

Barzak, Ibrahim. "Israel Rejects Militants' Ultimatum."

globeandmail.com. 3 July 2006. Web. 3 July 2006.

INTERNET SOURCE WITH NO AUTHOR

"Everything Postmodern." *Ebbflux*. Oct. 2004. Web. 3 July

2006.

E-MAIL

Chamberlain, Tim. "Re: Credibility in Magazines." Message to

the author. Web. 12 Nov. 2006. E-mail.

MISCELLANEOUS SOURCES

GOVERNMENT PUBLICATION
If you do not know the author of the work, give the name of
the government, followed by the name of the agency.

Ontario. Ontario Human Rights Commission. *Human Rights:*

Employment Application Forms and Interview. Toronto:

Ontario Human Rights Commission, 1991. Print.

If you know the author's name, you may put it either at the
beginning of the entry or after the title, preceded by *By* or an
abbreviation such as *Ed.* or *Comp.*

PAMPHLET
Use the same format as that of a book entry.

Canada. Revenue Canada. Customs, Excise and Taxation.

Basics for Self-Employed Craftspeople. Ottawa:

Revenue Canada, 1993. Print.

DISSERTATION
PUBLISHED DISSERTATION

Haas, Arthur G. *Metternich, Reorganization and Nationality,*

1813–1818. Diss. U of Chicago, 1963. Knoxville: U of

Tennessee P, 1964. Print.

UNPUBLISHED DISSERTATION

Mercer, Todd. "Perspective, Point of View, and Perception:

James Joyce and Fredric Jameson." Diss. U of Victoria,

1987. Print.

PUBLISHED PROCEEDINGS OF A CONFERENCE
Treat as you would a book, but give any additional information about the conference.

Cassidy, Frank, ed. *Proceedings of Land Claims in British*

Columbia Conference, February 21–22, 1990: Reaching

Just Settlements. Lantzville and Halifax: Oolichan and

Inst. for Research on Public Policy, 1991. Print.

LECTURE OR PUBLIC ADDRESS
Give the speaker's name, the title of the presentation in quotation marks, the name of the sponsoring organization, the location, and the date.

Hill, Larry. "Navigating the Void and Developing a Sense of

Identity." Traill College, Trent University, Peterborough.

30 Jan. 2002. Address.

CD-ROM

The Rosetta Stone. Harrisburg: Fairfield Language

Technologies, 1995. CD-ROM.

"Einstein, Albert." *The 1995 Grolier Multimedia Encyclopedia*.

Danbury: Grolier, 1997. CD-ROM.

MUSICAL COMPOSITION

Give the composer's name, then the title of the work. Italicize the title unless the form, number, and key are used to identify the composition; in that case, do not italicize or use quotation marks. You may add the date of composition after the title.

Mozart, Wolfgang Amadeus. *The Marriage of Figaro*. 1786.

Mozart, Wolfgang Amadeus. Piano Concerto in B Flat.

Published scores are treated like books.

Beethoven, Ludwig van. *Symphony No. 7 in A, Op. 92*. 1768.

New York: Dover, 1998. Print.

SOUND RECORDING

Which person you list first (composer, conductor, or performer) depends on what aspect of the recording you wish to empha-size. Give the title of a specific song in quotation marks and the title of the recording in italics. Next give the names of other art-ists. End with the manufacturer and year of issue, separated by a comma. Periods follow all other items. Note the medium.

Verdi, Guiseppe. *Arias*. Perf. Simon Estes. New Philharmonic

Orchestra. Cond. Gaetano Delogu. Philips, 1987. LP.

The Band. "It Makes No Difference." *The Best of the Band*.

Capitol, 1976. Audiocassette.

PERFORMANCE

Give the title, italicized, followed by the names of contributors such as the playwright, choreographer, director, or performers, preceded by *By*, *Chor.*, *Dir.*, or *Perf.* as appropriate. Then give the site of the performance: usually the theatre name, followed by a comma, then the city, followed by a period. Conclude with the date of the performance and the medium.

> *Indian Ink*. By Tom Stoppard. Dir. Richard Cottrell. Perf. Fiona
>
> Reid. Bluma Appel Theatre, Toronto. 1 Apr. 2002.
>
> Performance.

FILM OR VIDEO

Give the title, italicized, followed by the name of the director, preceded by *Dir.* You may also name the writer, performers, narrator, or producer, preceded by the appropriate abbreviation. Then give the distributor and year of release and the medium.

> *Othello*. Dir. Stuart Burge. Perf. Laurence Olivier, Maggie
>
> Smith, Joyce Redman, and Frank Finlay. Warner
>
> Brothers, 1965. Film.

For a video recording, include the original release date if applicable. Give the distributor's name and the year the video was released, then add the appropriate label or abbreviation, for example, *Videocassette* or *DVD*, for the medium.

> *The Big Snit*. Dir. Richard Condie. National Film Board of
>
> Canada, 1985. DVD.
>
> *Suspicion*. Dir. Alfred Hitchcock. Perf. Cary Grant and Joan
>
> Fontaine. 1941. Turner, 1995. Laser disc.

RADIO OR TELEVISION PROGRAM

Give the title of the episode in quotation marks, then the title of the program in italics. If applicable and relevant, give the name of the writer, narrator, producer, and/or performer(s), preceded by *By*, *Narr.*, *Prod.*, or *Perf.* Give the series (if any) and the network, separated by a comma. Finish with the date of the broadcast and the medium.

> "A Hail of Bullets." *The Fifth Estate*. CBC Newsworld. 7 July
>
> 2006. Television.

"Second City: First Family of Comedy." *Life and Times*. CBC

Newsworld. 25 Aug. 2006. Television.

"Ravel's Brain." Dir. Larry Weinstein. *Sunday Encore*. CBC. 9

July 2006. Television.

INTERVIEW
Give the name of the person interviewed, followed by the title of the interview, if any, usually in quotation marks. If there is no title, use the label *Interview* after the name of the person interviewed, followed by *with* and the name of the interviewer, if relevant. Then give publication or broadcast information.

Bellow, Saul. "Treading on the Toes of Brahmans."

Endangered Species: Writers Talk about Their Craft,

Their Visions, Their Lives. By Lawrence Grobel.

Cambridge, MA: Da Capo, 2001. 1–60. Print.

Brumlik, Micha. Interview with Rick MacInnes-Rae. *The*

Current. CBC Radio One. 5 July 2006. Radio.

If you cite information from an interview you have conducted, give the name of the person interviewed, followed by a description, such as *Personal interview, Telephone interview,* or *E-mail interview,* and the date.

Robertson, Robbie. Personal interview. 5 July 2006.

FINE ART
Give the artist's full name, then the title of the work, italicized. Then name the institution (or owner) and the city. You may add the date of origin immediately after the title.

Weiland, Joyce. *Défendez la Terre/Defend the Earth*. 1972–73.

National Science Library, Ottawa.

For a photograph of a work of art, follow the example above and add the publication information for the source containing the photograph.

CARTOON

Give the artist's name, the title of the cartoon or comic (if any) in quotation marks, the descriptive label *Cartoon* or *Comic strip*, the publication information, and medium.

> Moudakis, Theo. Cartoon. *Toronto Star* 4 July 2006: A14.
>
> Print.

PERSONAL LETTER

Give the letter writer's name, followed by *Letter to the author*, the date, and the medium.

> Helm, Levon. Letter to the author. 5 July 2006. TS.

MAP OR CHART

Treat as you would an anonymous book, adding the label *Map* or *Chart* as appropriate.

> *Great Britain/Scotland 501*. Map. Paris: Michelin, 2011. Print.

Information Notes

Two types of optional information notes may be used with parenthetical documentation.

1. **Content notes** give the reader additional information that would have interrupted the flow of ideas in the text. They should be brief.
2. **Bibliographic notes** provide evaluative commentary on sources and may be used for references containing numerous citations.

To create an information note, place a superscript Arabic number at the appropriate place in the text and insert a matching numeral either at the bottom of the page (footnote) or on a separate page at the end of the paper (endnote) before the Works Cited page.

Try to organize your sentence so the need for an information note falls at the end of the sentence. Give the end-of-sentence punctuation followed by the raised (superscript) note number. Information notes should be numbered consecutively throughout a paper or throughout a chapter of a book.

When writing a footnote or endnote, indent the first line, then put the number, followed by a period and a space. Do not indent any line after the first one. Double-space within and between notes.

Circumnavigation of any large land body in a kayak requires significant, time-consuming preparation.[1] The catastrophic effects of inadequate equipment or ill-prepared participants have been well documented in recent testimonials.[2]

1. For a full discussion of the preparation required, see Fenger 32.
2. Foremost among these are the stories of Smith and Patterson, the Ontario Kayak Club, and Michael Summers.

Manuscript Format

The following sections detail the current MLA specifications for formatting a research paper. Check with your instructor to find out if there are any additional or alternative requirements for a particular assignment.

MATERIALS AND TYPEFACE

For academic writing, use good-quality, white, letter-size (22 × 28 cm, or 8.5 × 11 in.) paper. If possible, use a high-quality printer. Make sure your printer cartridge is new enough to create distinct and—above all—readable text. Print on one side of the paper only. Many instructors prefer that you use a paper clip rather than a folder or binder; some may want the paper stapled. Keep a spare copy of any paper you submit (ideally, both a hard copy and an electronic backup).

Ensure that your paper is easy to read by using one of the standard book typefaces, such as Times New Roman, and use 12-point font. Do not justify the text; it should be ragged right.

TITLE

MLA does not require a title page. Your name, your instructor's name, the course number, and the date appear at the top of the first page, flush with the left margin and double-spaced. The title is centred two lines below the date. In the title, capitalize the first word, the last word, and all principal words, including those that follow hyphens, but not articles, prepositions, coordinating conjunctions, or the to in infinitives. The title is not underlined or in italics or quotation marks and is not followed by a period. Double-space after the title and indent 1.25 cm (0.5 in.) at the beginning of the first line of the text.

MARGINS AND SPACING

Leave margins of 2.5 cm (1 in.) on the top, bottom, and both sides of the page unless your instructor requires a larger margin for marking purposes.

Double-space everything in the paper, including quotations, notes, and the list of works cited. Leave one space after a period or other punctuation mark, but do not space before or after a dash or between the two hyphens that may be used to compose a dash.

Indent the first line of each paragraph 1.25 cm (0.5 in.) from the left margin.

For quotations of more than four lines of prose or more than three lines of poetry, indent 2.5 cm (1 in.) from the left margin without adding quotation marks. Introduce the quotation with a colon.

PAGE NUMBERS

Number all pages consecutively in the upper right-hand corner, 1.25 cm (0.5 in.) from the top of the page and flush with the right margin. Use only Arabic numerals and place your last name before every page number. You can use your word-processing program to create a header with your name and page number that will automatically appear on every page. Do not use the abbreviation *p.* or include hyphens or parentheses.

Another source you might consult for more detailed information about MLA format and documentation style is the *MLA Style Manual and Guide to Scholarly Publishing* (3rd ed., 2008).

SAMPLE PAPER: MLA STYLE

The following pages, taken from a university student's paper, illustrate some important features of MLA style.

Dan McKeown

Dr. S. O'Brien

English 4W03

26 February 2007

Title is centred and double-spaced.

"The White Man's Burden" and Characterization in

E. M. Forster's *A Passage to India*

Nobel Prize winner V. S. Naipaul claims that E. M. Forster knew hardly anything about India: "He just knew a few middle-class Indians and the garden boys whom he wished to seduce" (*E. M. Forster*). Yet Forster demonstrates that he knows a great deal about the cultural divide between the races in *A Passage to India*. Indeed, Forster uses his characters to show the impossibility of understanding Indians when one is limited to Victorian conceptions such as the "white man's burden."

The most fundamental way to describe "the white man's burden," especially in a historical-literary context, is to understand it as an extension of Edward Said's principle of Orientalism. In this view, Orientalism is a way of organizing and understanding "truths" about the East. The British, for example, establish and understand a system of knowledge about India by opposing the racial "truths" of "us" and "them" (Said 1279–80).

Citation includes author's name and page number(s) in parentheses.

Author is named in signal phrase; page number is given in parentheses at end of paraphrase.

When the British physically enter India, however, this knowledge must somehow be transferred from the British imagination and, in a sense, "re-projected" onto India so that it can be actualized in the operation of the Empire. As Said explains, the Westerner creates "a whole series of possible relationships with the Orient" without ever relinquishing his or her hegemony (1281). "The white man's burden" was one such relationship. Between the late nineteenth century and World War II, "the white man's burden" was the underlying ideology of Britain's Imperial relationship with India. Straightforward and relatively uniform in Britain, the "burden" was to "civilize" India. In India itself, however, the relationship was conflicted and certainly not uniform. As E. M. Forster demonstrates in *A Passage to India*, the main characters (British and Indian) of Chandrapore have highly conflicted views about the role of the white man in India. Ultimately, Forster uses his characters to demonstrate the impossibility of engaging Orientalist "truths" about Indians via "the white man's burden."

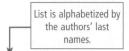

List is alphabetized by the authors' last names.

List of works cited begins on a separate page.

Works Cited

Armstrong, Paul. "Reading India: E. M. Forster and the Politics of Interpretation." *Twentieth-Century Literature: A Scholarly and Critical Journal* 18.4 (1992): 365–85. Print.

Edward Morgan Forster (1879–1970). Web. 30 Jan. 2007.

Forster, E. M. *A Passage to India*. London: Penguin, 1979. Print.

Heath, Jeffrey. "A Voluntary Surrender: Imperialism and Imagination in *A Passage to India*." *U of Toronto Quarterly* 59 (1998–99): 287–309. Print.

Kipling, Rudyard. "The White Man's Burden." *The Writings in Prose and Verse of Rudyard Kipling*. Vol. 21. New York: Scribner's, 1903. Print. 36 vols.

Lawrence, James. "The White Man's Burden? Imperial Wars in the 1890s." *History Today* 42 (1992): 45–51. Print.

Lin, Lidan. "The Irony of Colonial Humanism." *Review of International English Literature* 28 (1997): 133–53. Print.

Loeb, Kurt. *White Man's Burden*. Toronto: Lugus, 1992. Print.

Meyers, Jeffrey. *Fiction and the Colonial Experience*. New Jersey: Rowman, 1973. Print.

Said, Edward. "From the Introduction to Orientalism." *The Critical Tradition*. Ed. David Richter. Boston: Bedford, 1998. 1278–92. Print.

Van Creveld, Martin. *The Rise and Decline of the State*. Cambridge: Cambridge UP, 1999. Print.

Each entry is a hanging indent, where the first line is typed flush left.

APA STYLE OF DOCUMENTATION

Writers in the social sciences generally follow the American Psychological Association guidelines for formatting and documenting sources. When following APA style, you document your sources in two ways:

1. Within the body of the paper, using **in-text citations**
2. At the end of the paper, in a **list of references**

In-Text Citations

APA style uses the author-date method of citation, giving the author and date of publication in parentheses within the essay. Each of these parenthetical citations has a matching entry giving complete publication information in the *References* list on a separate page at the end of the essay. If a specific part of a source is paraphrased or quoted, the citation also includes the page number (or chapter, figure, table, or equation), as detailed below.

FORMAT OF CITATIONS FOR PRINT SOURCES

ONE AUTHOR
Give the name and the year of publication in parentheses, separated by a comma.

> One study (Woods, 2006) cast some doubt on the efficacy of the procedure.

If the name of the author is given in a signal phrase, cite only the year of publication in parentheses.

> As Bayly (2006) clearly demonstrates, the technical excellence of the procedure resulted in long wait times for patients.

If both the author and the year are given in a signal phrase, do not add parenthetical information.

> Fawcett's seminal 2006 study showed that the data had been doctored to illustrate the desired result.

SPECIFIC PART OF A SOURCE
To cite quotations or paraphrased information taken from a precise location in a work, follow the guidelines above but also give a location reference, such as the page number or the chapter, figure, table, or equation. Abbreviate *page* (*p.*), *pages* (*pp.*), but not *chapter*.

Peter Newman (1995, p. 183) observes, "As the institutional touchstones that had once been the nation's Pole Star fell away, Canadians began automatically to distrust anyone who exercised authority over their lives."

One observer notes, "As the institutional touchstones that had once been the nation's Pole Star fell away, Canadians began automatically to distrust anyone who exercised authority over their lives" (Newman, 1995, p. 183).

TWO AUTHORS

Cite both names along with the year of publication. If the names appear in a signal phrase, join them with *and*; in a parenthetical reference, use the ampersand (&).

Clarkson and McCall (1990) agree that Trudeau's writings during the early 1960s revealed him at the height of his powers as a writer and Quebec theoretician on federalism.

During the early 1960s, Trudeau was at the height of his powers as a writer and was viewed as the preeminent Quebec theoretician on federalism (Clarkson & McCall, 1990).

THREE TO FIVE AUTHORS

Give the names of all the authors only in the first citation; remember to use the ampersand (&) instead of *and*. In subsequent citations, give only the first author's last name and the abbreviation *et al.* (not italicized and with a period after *al.*).

First Citation of the Source

Effective class groups do not happen randomly; however, an instructor can encourage their development by employing effective teaching methods and monitoring group performance (Lang, McBeath, & Hebert, 1995).

Subsequent Citation of the Source

Classroom management approaches can be classified according to the degree of teacher intervention and the control each approach needs (Lang et al., 1995).

SIX OR MORE AUTHORS

Many assert that Canada's involvement in World War I was characterized by racism in some instances and by greed and corruption in others (Newman et al., 2000).

NO AUTHOR

Cite the first few words of the title along with the year. Italicize titles of books, magazines, journals, and reports. Use quotation marks around titles of articles or chapters.

> One recent report ("UN Guns," 2006) suggests that the UN conference on the illicit gun trade ended in disarray, with weaker results than in 2001.

CORPORATE AUTHOR

Entry in Reference List: Assembly of First Nations. (2006).
First Citation: (Assembly of First Nations [AFN], 2006)
Subsequent Citations: (AFN, 2006)

TWO OR MORE WORKS IN A SINGLE CITATION

Give the sources in alphabetical order by the authors' last names. Separate the citations with a semicolon.

> Researchers have concluded that there is no point in searching for a single creativity score comparable to an IQ score (Halpern, 1984; Rothstein, 1990).

Two or more works by the same author(s) are arranged by year of publication, with commas separating the years. If two or more works by the same author(s) have the same publication date, distinguish the works by adding *a*, *b*, *c*, and so on after the year.

> (Nichol, 1984, 1986, 1987a, 1987b)

PERSONAL COMMUNICATION

For letters, memos, e-mails, interviews, and telephone conversations, give the initials and last name of the communicator and the date on which the communication took place. Because they are not verifiable, personal communications are not included in the *References* list.

> J. Nadler (personal communication, November 12, 2006) indicated that the Russian mafia played a significant role in supplying protection for Budapest nightclub owners.

FORMAT OF CITATIONS FOR ELECTRONIC SOURCES

Follow the guidelines for print sources but add location information to direct the reader to a specific part of the source. For an electronic source with no page numbers, use the paragraph number if it is available, preceded by the abbreviation *para.* and a space.

As Myers (2000, para. 7) aptly phrased it, "positive emotions are both an end—better to live fulfilled, with joy [and other positive emotions]—and a means to a more caring and healthy society."

If neither paragraph nor page numbers are available, cite the heading and the number of the paragraph following it.

Panic disorder currently affects six million American adults (NIMH, 2006, Panic Disorder, para. 6).

If no page numbers, paragraph numbers, or headings are provided, it may be necessary to omit a location reference.

List of References

For every citation in the text of your paper, there must be a matching entry in a list of references at the end of the paper. Only sources used in the research and preparation of the paper are included in the *References* list.

The following section presents guidelines for setting up a list of references and model entries for common types of sources. If the source you have used in your research paper is not described in this section, consult the *Publication Manual of the American Psychological Association*, 6th ed. (Washington: APA, 2010). Some tips and guidelines are also available on the APA website at www.apastyle.org.

ARRANGEMENT OF ENTRIES

All sources that you used for your research paper and cited in the text must be listed alphabetically in your *References* list.

Alphabetize entries by the authors' surnames.

If no author is given, or if there is a group author, such as an agency, association, or institution, alphabetize by the first significant word of the name. Do not consider initial articles—*A*, *An*, or *The*—when you alphabetize. Use full official names rather than abbreviations.

ELEMENTS OF ENTRIES

AUTHOR

Invert all author names. Give the last name, followed by a comma, and then the initial(s)—do not use the full first name.

When there are two or more authors, use the ampersand (&) rather than the word *and*. Separate author names with commas, including before an ampersand.

For an edited book, place the name of the editor or editors in the author position, followed by the abbreviation *Ed.* or *Eds.* in parentheses.

If the reference has no author, move the title to the author position.

For references with more than seven authors, insert three ellipsis point after the sixth author's name, followed by the last author's name.

The author element of the entry should end with a period; if it closes with a parenthesis—for example, with (Ed.)—add a period after the closing parenthesis. If an author's initial with a period ends the element, do not add an extra period.

PUBLICATION DATE

Place the publication date in parentheses after the last author's (or editor's) name.

For a published work, give the year the work was copyrighted; for an unpublished work, give the year it was produced.

For magazines, newsletters, or newspapers, give the year, followed by the exact date of publication as it appears on the issue: the month or months, the season, or the month and day. Spell the names of months in full.

If no date is given, place *n.d.* in parentheses. For articles accepted for publication but not yet published, write *in press* in parentheses.

Finish the date element of the entry with a period after the closing parenthesis.

TITLE OF ARTICLE OR CHAPTER

Do not italicize or underline article or chapter titles or place them within quotation marks.

Capitalize only the first word of the title and of the subtitle and any proper nouns.

After the article title, other identifying information may be included in brackets, for example, [*Letter to the editor*] or [*Abstract*].

Finish the element with a period.

TITLE OF WORK AND PUBLICATION INFORMATION

NON-PERIODICALS

For a non-periodical, such as a book, after the author name(s) and date, give the following information: title of work; additional information, such as edition; a description of the form of the work if applicable; place of publication; publisher.

TITLE: Italicize book titles and subtitles. Capitalize only the first word of the title and of the subtitle, as well as any proper nouns. End the title with a period, unless you will be adding additional information (see next item).

ADDITIONAL INFORMATION: Give edition, report number, or volume number, if applicable, in parentheses immediately after the title. Do not use a period between the title and the parenthetical information and do not italicize.

Following any parenthetical information, give a description of the form of the work, if necessary, enclosed in brackets—for example, [*Brochure*] or [*Videotape*]. End with a period.

PLACE OF PUBLICATION: Give the city where the work was published. If the city could be confused with another location, also give the state or province and, if necessary, the country. Use two-letter postal abbreviations for states and provinces. Use a colon to separate the place of publication from the publisher's name.

PUBLISHER: Give the publisher's name as briefly as possible, omitting words and abbreviations such as *Publishers*, *Co.*, and Inc. but retaining the words *Books* and *Press*. End with a period.

PART OF A NON-PERIODICAL: When referencing part of a non-periodical, such as a book chapter, give the author, date, and chapter title as described above, and then add the following elements:

1. The word *In* followed by the editor's name, not inverted, followed by the abbreviation *Ed*. in parentheses. If there is no editor, simply include the word *In* followed by the title of the work.
2. The title of the work in italics
3. Inclusive page numbers for the chapter, in parentheses and preceded by the abbreviation *pp*.
4. The publication information as outlined above

PERIODICALS

After the author(s), date, and title of article, additional information appears in the following order: periodical name, volume number (if applicable), issue number (if applicable), and inclusive page numbers.

PERIODICAL NAME: Give the complete name, in italics, followed by a comma.

VOLUME NUMBER: Give the volume number, if any, in italics. Do not use Vol. before the volume number. Place a comma after the volume number unless it is followed by an issue number. If there is no volume number, include the month or season with the year, for example, (*2006, September*).

ISSUE NUMBER: If each issue of the periodical begins on page 1, give the issue number in parentheses immediately after the volume number, leaving no space, followed by a comma.

PAGE NUMBERS: Give inclusive page numbers after the volume (or issue) number. Use the abbreviations *p.* or *pp.* for newspaper articles but not for magazine or journal articles.

EXAMPLES OF REFERENCES ENTRIES

BOOKS
ONE AUTHOR

> McConnell, J. (1974). *Understanding human behavior: An*
>
> *introduction to psychology*. New York, NY: Holt,
>
> Rinehart.

TWO OR MORE AUTHORS

> Krebs, D., & Blackman, R. (1988). *Psychology: A first*
>
> *encounter*. San Diego, CA: Harcourt.

> Griffin, R. W., Ebert, R. J., & Starke, F. A. (1999). *Business* (3rd
>
> Canadian ed.). Scarborough, ON: Prentice Hall.

EDITED BOOK

> Fraser, K. (Ed.). (1991). *Bad trips*. Toronto, ON: Random House.

TRANSLATION

> Barthes, R. (1987). *Mythologies* (A. Lavers, Trans.). London,
>
> England: Paladin Grafton Books. (Original work pub-
>
> lished 1957.)

CORPORATE AUTHOR

> Ministry of Education and Training. (1990). *Ministry of*
>
> *Education and Training style guide for editors and*
>
> *writers*. Toronto, ON: Author.

No Author or Editor

German for travellers. (1986). Lausanne, Switzerland: Editions

Berlitz.

Subsequent Editions

Gifford, D. (1982). *Joyce annotated* (2nd ed.). Berkeley, CA:

University of California Press.

Multivolume Work

Mansion, J. E. (1974). *Harrap's new standard French and*

English dictionary (Vols. 1–2). London, England: Harrap.

Article in an Edited Book

Bruce, H. (1988). Portugal. In K. Dobbs (Ed.), *Away from*

home: Canadian writers in exotic places (pp. 297–301).

Toronto, ON: Deneau.

Article in a Reference Book

Watkins, C. (1998). Indo-European and the Indo-Europeans. In

Canadian dictionary of the English language (pp. 1631–

1637). Toronto, ON: ITP Nelson.

PERIODICALS
Article in a Journal Paginated by Volume

Dodd, D. (2001). Helen MacMurchy, MD: Gender and profes-

sional conflict in the medical inspection of Toronto

schools, 1910–1911. *Ontario History, 93,* 127–149.

Article in a Journal Paginated by Issue

Martin, R. (2002). The virtue matrix: Calculating the return on

corporate responsibility. *Harvard Business Review,*

80(3), 69–75.

Article in a Magazine

Tarry, C. (2002, March). The Danube: Europe's river of har-

mony and discord. *National Geographic, 201*, 62–79.

Article in a Newspaper

MacGregor, K. (2002, March 12). Zimbabwe voting ends in

confusion. *The Globe and Mail*, p. A14.

Anonymous Article

Newsmakers. (2006, February 6). *Maclean's, 119*(1), 44–45.

Letter to the Editor

Marajh, T. (2002, March 12). Father was following natural love

[Letter to the editor]. *The Toronto Star*, p. A27.

Review

Chodoff, P. (2002). Redeeming Frieda [Review of the book *To*

redeem one person is to redeem the world: The life of

Frieda Fromm-Reichmann, by G. A. Hornstein].

Psychology Today, 35, 76.

ELECTRONIC SOURCES

As with any reference, the goals of referencing electronic
sources are to give credit to the author and to allow the reader
to find the source material with the least effort.

At a minimum, a reference for an Internet source should
include the author name(s) if possible, the title or a description

of the document, a publication date, date of retrieval (if source material may change), and an exact address (URL).

The date should indicate the year of publication or, if the source undergoes regular revision, the most recent update. If the document has no date, put *n.d.* in parentheses after the first element (author or title) and then the URL (e.g., *Retrieved from* http://www.apa.org).

The retrieval statement containing an exact address replaces the publication information typically provided for print references. Help readers locate information by being as specific as possible. As well as the host name, include the protocol (*http, ftp, gopher, telnet, news*) and any relevant path and file names. If a URL runs over a line, break it only after a slash or before a period and make sure no hyphens are inadvertently added at line breaks. No final period appears after the end of the URL, and the URL is not placed in angle brackets.

If there is a DOI (otherwise known as a digital object identifier), include it at the end of the reference in place of the URL (e.g., doi:10.1037/0278-6133.24.2.225). Do not put a period at the end of the DOI. To search for the citation of an item by its DOI, visit www.doi.org. Since electronic media change rapidly, check the APA website or www.owl.english.purdue.edu/owl/resource/560/10 for regularly updated information about documenting electronic sources.

ARTICLE BASED ON A PRINT SOURCE
Often, articles retrieved from online publications are exact duplicates of print versions. In these cases, follow the format of the print form.

> Strain, L. A. (2000). Seniors' centres: Who cares? *Canadian*
>
> *Journal of Aging, 20*, 471–491.

If the online article and the print article differ (e.g., if page numbers are not included or additional information is given), add the URL.

> Sands, P. (2002, Fall). Pushing and pulling toward the middle.
>
> *Kairos, 7*(3). Retrieved from http://technorhetoric
>
> .org/7.3/coverweb.html

INTERNET-ONLY JOURNAL
Reference as in the preceding example. However, if no volume or issue numbers are used, simply provide the name of the periodical, the retrieval date, and the URL.

Smith, J. (2003, January 16). Journalism fails its sobriety test.

Salon. Retrieved from http://www.salon.com/2003/01/

16/dui_3/

STAND-ALONE DOCUMENT, NO AUTHOR IDENTIFIED, NO DATE

Begin the reference with the title of the document.

Erikson's development stages. (n.d.). Retrieved from http://

www2.honolulu.hawaii.edu/facdev/guidebk/teachtip/

erikson.htm

ONLINE DISCUSSION SOURCES

Often, newsgroups, forums, discussion groups, and electronic mailing lists are not referenced because they are not peer reviewed and posts are not retrievable. If the source is archived, cite the author's name and the exact date of online posting. Follow this with the subject line of the message and the description of the form in brackets. Follow this with the URL and provide the name of the list if this is not included in the URL.

Nivalainen, M. (2002, December 17). The key and stupid web

moments of 2002. [Electronic mailing list message.]

Retrieved from www.http://www.shift.com/print/

10.5/432/1.html

ARTICLE RETRIEVED FROM A DATABASE

Use the appropriate format for the source, adding the retrieval date and the name of the database.

Lindblad, F., Lindberg, L., & Hjern, A. (2006, July 6). Anorexia

nervosa in young men: A cohort study. International

Journal of Eating Disorders. Retrieved from PubMed

database.

DOCUMENT ON A UNIVERSITY WEBSITE

For a document on a large and complex website (e.g., a university or government site), identify the host organization and the relevant program or department before giving the URL for the document itself.

> Megginson, D. (1996). Noun and pronoun characteristics.
>
> University of Ottawa, The Writing Centre. Retrieved
>
> from http://www.writingcentre.uottawa.ca/
>
> hypergrammar/nounchar.html

E-MAIL

Since e-mail messages are not retrievable by the reader, they should not be included in a reference list. They may be cited in the text as a personal communication.

MISCELLANEOUS SOURCES

MUSIC RECORDING

> Manuel, R. (1968). Lonesome Suzie. [Recorded by The Band].
>
> On *Music from Big Pink* [CD]. Hollywood, CA: Capitol.
>
> (2003).

TELEVISION BROADCAST

> Burman, T. (Executive Producer). (2003, October 5). *The*
>
> *national* [Television broadcast]. Toronto, ON: Canadian
>
> Broadcasting Corporation.

SINGLE EPISODE FROM A TELEVISION SERIES

> Ferrand, C. (Director). (2006, February 11). Arctic mission:
>
> People of the ice. [Television series episode]. In M.
>
> Allder (Executive producer), *The nature of things with*

David Suzuki. Toronto, ON: Canadian Broadcasting

Corporation.

MOTION PICTURE

Anderson, W., Mendel, B., & Rudin, S. (Producers), &

Anderson, W. (Director). (2001). *The Royal Tenenbaums*

[Motion picture]. United States: Touchstone Pictures.

DISSERTATION ABSTRACT

Karim, Y. (1999). Arab political dispute mediations.

Dissertation Abstracts International, 61, 350.

GOVERNMENT DOCUMENT

Solicitor General of Canada. (1995). Annual report on the use

of electronic surveillance. Ottawa: Author.

CONFERENCE PROCEEDINGS PUBLISHED IN A BOOK

Chorney, H. (1991). A regional approach to monetary and

fiscal policy. In J. N. McCrorie & M. L. MacDonald (Eds.),

The Constitutional future of the Prairie and Atlantic

regions of Canada (pp. 107–121). Regina, SK: Canadian

Plains Research Center Press.

Note that regularly published conference proceedings are treated as periodicals.

Manuscript Format

MATERIALS AND TYPEFACE

Use letter-size (22 × 28 cm, 8.5 × 11 in.), paper, and print on one side only.

Use a standard serif typeface, such as Times New Roman, in 12-point size. Avoid typefaces that are unusual or too small. A serif typeface is preferable because it enhances readability and reduces eyestrain. The type on the paper must be dark, clear, and easy to photocopy.

TITLE AND IDENTIFICATION

Although APA style does not give specific guidelines for formatting a title page for college and university papers, the example that follows is typical of the format most instructors require. Check with your instructor for the format you should use.

MARGINS, SPACING, AND INDENTATION

Leave margins of at least 2.5 cm (1 in.) at the top, bottom, left, and right sides of every page.

Double-space the text throughout, including the title, headings, quotations, footnotes, figure captions, and all parts of tables. Text should be ragged right rather than right justified. Do not divide words at the end of a line or use the hyphenation feature of your word-processing software.

Indent the first line of every paragraph 1.25 cm (0.5 in.). APA style specifies that quotations of 40 or more words should be further indented by 1.25 cm (0.5 in.) and double-spaced, without an opening paragraph indent and without quotation marks.

PAGE NUMBERS AND SHORT TITLES

Number all pages consecutively, beginning with the title page, placing Arabic numerals in the upper right-hand corner at least 2.5 cm (1 in.) from the right side of the page and 1.25 cm (0.5 in.) from the top.

On the same line as the page number, but set flush with the left margin, include an abbreviated title—the first two or three words of the full title. This shortened title will identify pages should they become separated. APA, in its guidelines for manuscript preparation, does not recommend putting your name on each page.

PUNCTUATION

APA guidelines call for one space after a period or any other punctuation mark. To create a dash, type two hyphens (--) with no spaces before or after. You may also use your word-processing software to create a dash (—).

ABSTRACT

Your instructor may ask you to include an abstract—a brief summary of your research paper. An abstract appears separately on page 2 and is one paragraph, double-spaced, and typed as a block without indentation. The maximum length for an abstract varies from 150 to 250 words, and it can be considerably less. It is meant to provide a summary of your paper, including your thesis and the main points of your research. It should also suggest what your research implies and how it might be applied. Centre the heading *Abstract* over the paragraph.

HEADINGS

Headings are encouraged in APA style. They define the hierarchy of ideas and help the reader understand the structure and organization of the paper.

The APA guidelines for formatting headings are as follows:

Main Headings: centred, boldface, uppercase and lowercase (first letter of important words capitalized)

Second-Level Headings: flush left, boldface, uppercase and lowercase

Third-Level Headings: indented, boldface, lowercase paragraph heading (with initial capital) ending with a period

VISUALS

In APA style, any type of illustration other than a table—including charts, graphs, drawings, and photographs—is called a figure. While tables are preferred for the presentation of quantitative data, figures are used to convey structural or pictorial concepts. Use the following guidelines to identify illustrations.

TABLES

Above the table, number consecutively with Arabic numerals. Give the title of the table in italics, double-spaced.

Table 1

Univariate Analyses of Continuous Non-Academic Variables

FIGURES

Below the figure, number consecutively with Arabic numerals in italics, followed by a caption (no italics). The caption acts as both the title and an explanation of the figure.

Figure 1. Desired service response and links for young people

with mental health issues.

If you include a visual, make sure that it is mentioned and discussed in the body of your paper so the reader is alerted to its presence and its significance to your argument.

Tables and figures may appear in the body of a student paper rather than at the end. Ask your instructor for guidelines on the preferred placement.

DOCUMENTATION

Any sources you have used in the research and writing of your paper must be correctly documented according to APA guidelines.

Sample Paper

Daniel Rosenfield, a university student, wrote the following research paper as part of his requirements for a humanities course. Rosenfield's assignment was to review recent credible and reliable sources documenting stem cell research policies and regulations, then evaluate the effectiveness of those policies and regulations.

Rosenfield used the APA guidelines for manuscript formatting and documentation of sources that are presented in this handbook. His in-text citations follow APA style, as does his list of references. Rosenfield's instructor required that students provide a title page with their papers but not an abstract, since the paper was to be fairly short.

THE STATE, SCIENCE, AND STEM CELLS 1

Abbreviated title appears flush left on the same line as the page number, which is flush against the right margin. Page numbering begins on the title page.

The full title of the paper is typed in upper- and lowercase, double-spaced, and centred in the upper half of the title page.

The State, Science, and Stem Cells:

An Analysis of the American Stance on Stem Cell Research

Daniel Rosenfield

The author's name should be centred, and appears approximately midway down the page.

Health Sciences 3A03

Professor Gildiner

November 18, 2008

Centred in the bottom third of the page are the course number and section number, the instructor's name, and the date the paper was submitted.

> Include full title, centred, at the beginning of the essay.

The State, Science, and Stem Cells:

An Analysis of the American Stance on Stem Cell Research

Introduction

> Headings are commonly used in APA style. Because this essay is short, it uses a Level 2 heading throughout. You may need a more elaborate hierarchy of headings if your work is long or complex.

In the United States and around the world, a growing debate is emerging surrounding the regulation of new biotechnologies. With cloning, gene manipulation, and stem cell research all blossoming, the need for government intervention and regulation is becoming increasingly clear. In this paper, I will focus on the regulation of stem cell research in the United States, and the debates surrounding policy. Specifically, I will highlight the debate around whether or not stem cells should be regulated, and if so, to what degree. I will also draw attention to the role of the state and various civil groups in determining stem cell research policies.

A Brief History

The debate surrounding stem cells is a relatively recent one, as the first isolation of embryonic stem cells was announced at the University of Wisconsin in 1998 (Knowles, 2004). However, after stem cells were identified, a flurry of controversy arose due to various ideologies presenting their views on the nature of embryos, and the sanctity of life. This was contrasted with the optimism of many scientists, who saw seemingly endless healing possibilities with stem cells.[1] Policy makers in the United States recognized the need to develop guidelines for the utilization and creation of stem cells, as well as their regulation. In addition, rules regarding the use of federal funds for stem cell research would have to be created and/or altered.

> Parenthetical (in-text) citations demand the author's name, if it is not mentioned in the text in a signal phrase, and the date.

> Superscript is used to indicate explanatory endnotes, listed at the end of the paper for simplicity of formatting.

References begin on a new page with this heading.

References

Baylis, F. (2002). Betwixt and between human stem cell guidelines and legislation. *Health Law Review, 11*(1), 44–50.

Brainard, J. (2005). National Academies report recommends tighter rules for stem-cell research. *Chronicle of Higher Education, 51*(35), A25.

Childress, J. F. (2004). Human stem cell research: Some controversies in bioethics and public policy. *Blood Cells, Molecules and Diseases, 32*(1), 100–105.

Fischbach, G. D., & Fischbach, R. L. (2004). Stem cells: Science, policy, and ethics. *Journal of Clinical Investigation, 114*(10), 1364–1370.

Frist, B. (2001). The promise and peril of embryonic stem cell research: A call for vigilant oversight. *Yale Journal of Health Policy, Law, and Ethics, 2*(1), 109, 167–176.

Fukuyama, F. (2003a). Policies for the future. In *Our posthuman future: Consequences of the biotechnology revolution* (pp. 203–218). London: Macmillan.

Fukuyama, F. (2003b). The political control of biotechnology. In *Our posthuman future: Consequences of the biotechnology revolution* (pp. 181–194). London: Macmillan.

Fukuyama, F. (2005). Human biomedicine and the problem of governance. *Perspectives in Biology and Medicine, 48*(2), 195–200.

Fukuyama, F., & Wagner, C. (2000). Information and biological revolutions: Global governance challenges—Summary of a study group. Washington: RAND.

Knowles, L. P. (2004). A regulatory patchwork—Human ES cell research oversight. *Nature and Biotechnology, 22*(2), 157–163.

Towns, C. R., & Jones, D. G. (2004). Stem cells: Public policy and ethics. *New Zealand Bioethics Journal, 5*(1), 22–28.

References are listed alphabetically by author's last name. First names are reduced to initials. Each entry appears as a hanging indent.

For two entries by the same author, list the author's name for each entry. If they are published in the same year, add the suffix *a, b, c,* and so on to the year of publication.

CHICAGO STYLE OF DOCUMENTATION

This chapter outlines the basic guidelines published in *The Chicago Manual of Style*, 16th ed. (Chicago: University of Chicago Press, 2010) and concludes with sample pages that follow Chicago format and documentation style.

The Chicago Manual of Style website (found at www.chicagomanualofstyle.org/home.html) also provides information on documentation style and format. For examples of cited materials, follow the "Tools" link. The "Chicago Style Q & A" page allows you to submit questions, and the "Search" bar helps you find what you need.

Chicago recommends two basic systems of documentation: (1) the author-date system and (2) the notes and bibliography system. The second style is what we will document here.

Notes and Bibliography System

Also called humanities style, this system is favoured by many writers in literature, history, and the arts. Notes (either endnotes or footnotes) are used instead of in-text citations. If the notes give full bibliographical information, the bibliography may be omitted. It is preferable, however, to give complete details in the bibliography, in which case the notes may be shortened to avoid unnecessary duplication. Check with your instructor to determine which approach is preferred and whether to format notes as footnotes or endnotes.

WITH A BIBLIOGRAPHY

All notes, including the first reference to a particular source, are shortened, giving the author's last name, a shortened version of the title, and the page number(s). Readers wanting additional information about the source will find it in the bibliography. Chicago recommends this practice because it minimizes duplication and is user-friendly and economical.

WITHOUT A BIBLIOGRAPHY

In a work without a full bibliography, the first citation of a particular source gives complete bibliographical information and subsequent references to that source are shortened.

NOTES

Notes can appear either together at the end of your research paper, as **endnotes**, or at the foot of the page on which the citation appears, as **footnotes**. Use the footnote or endnote function of your word-processing software to create notes. Note numbers should be placed at the end of a sentence or at the end of a clause, indicating that the information in that sentence or clause is from another source. When readers wish to locate specific source information, they can do so by locating the note with the corresponding number.

"The possibility of a Marxist literary theory," in the words of Frow, "is given in the promise and the ambiguity of the central Marxist metaphors relating the symbolic order to the social process."[1]

The note will be formatted in one of two ways, depending on whether or not the paper includes a bibliography. Here is the key used to identify the type of example shown in the following sections:

SN = shortened note

FN = full note

B = bibliography entry

IN A WORK WITH A BIBLIOGRAPHY

B Frow, John. *Marxism and Literary History.* Cambridge, MA: Harvard University Press, 1986.

Note that citations (even the first citation of a work) are shortened to avoid duplication of information given in the bibliography entry. Shortened notes typically include the author's last name, a condensed version of the title, and the page number.

SN 1. Frow, *Marxism*, 7.

IN A WORK WITHOUT A BIBLIOGRAPHY

The first note gives complete bibliographical information.

FN 1. John Frow, *Marxism and Literary History* (Cambridge, MA: Harvard University Press, 1986), 7.

Subsequent notes can be shortened.

SN 7. Frow, *Marxism*, 156.

If a work cited in two or more successive notes is identical, the abbreviation *ibid.* (from *ibidem*, "in the same place") may be used in place of the author/editor name, the title, and other identical information.

1. Frow, *Marxism*, 112–13.

2. Ibid.

3. Ibid., 132.

EXAMPLES OF NOTES AND BIBLIOGRAPHY ENTRIES

Entries in the following pages provide model notes and bibliographic entries for most of the types of resources you will use in your research. The following key identifies the example shown:

SN = shortened note

FN = full note

B = bibliographical entry

BOOKS
ONE AUTHOR

SN 1. Roberts, *Empire of the Soul*, 85.

FN 1. Paul William Roberts, *Empire of the Soul: Some Journeys in India* (Toronto: Stoddart, 1994), 85.

B Roberts, Paul William. *Empire of the Soul: Some Journeys in India*. Toronto: Stoddart, 1994.

TWO OR THREE AUTHORS

SN 2. Johnson and Blair, *Logical Self-Defence*, 17.

FN 2. Ralph H. Johnson and J. Anthony Blair, *Logical Self-Defence*, 2nd ed. (Toronto: McGraw-Hill Ryerson, 1983), 17.

B Johnson, Ralph H., and J. Anthony Blair. *Logical Self-Defence*. 2nd ed. Toronto: McGraw-Hill Ryerson, 1983.

Note that in the bibliographic entry, only the name of the first author is reversed and a comma precedes the and. Do not use an ampersand.

FOUR OR MORE AUTHORS

SN 3. Gini-Newman et al., *Echoes from the Past*, 168.

FN 3. Garfield Gini-Newman et al., *Echoes from the Past: World History to the Sixteenth Century* (Toronto: McGraw-Hill Ryerson, 2001), 168.

B Gini-Newman, Garfield, Elizabeth Graham, Rick Guisso, Elizabeth Mcluhan, Osman Mohamed, David Pendergast, James Reilly et al. *Echoes from the Past: World History to the Sixteenth Century*. Toronto: McGraw-Hill Ryerson, 2001.

This work has eleven authors. Chicago recommends that for ten authors or fewer, all should be listed in the bibliography. For eleven authors or more, only the first seven should be listed.

EDITED WORK WITHOUT AN AUTHOR

SN 4. Lamb and Arnold, *Reading*, 29.

FN 4. Pose Lamb and Richard Arnold, eds., *Reading: Foundations and Instructional Strategies* (Belmont, CA: Wadsworth, 1976), 29.

B Lamb, Pose, and Richard Arnold, eds. *Reading: Foundations and Instructional Strategies*. Belmont, CA: Wadsworth, 1976.

Note that the abbreviation *ed.* or *eds.* is omitted in shortened notes.

EDITED WORK WITH AN AUTHOR

SN 5. Mill, *On Liberty*, 45–46.

FN 5. John Stuart Mill, *On Liberty*, ed. Currin V. Shields (New York: Macmillan, 1956), 45–46.

B Mill, John Stuart. *On Liberty*. Edited by Currin V. Shields. New York: Macmillan, 1956.

Note that *Edited by* is spelled out in a bibliography but abbreviated in notes.

TRANSLATED WORK

SN 6. Sartre, *Iron in the Soul*, 58.

FN 6. Jean-Paul Sartre, *Iron in the Soul*, trans. Gerard Hopkins (Harmondsworth, UK: Penguin Books, 1978), 58.

B Sartre, Jean-Paul. *Iron in the Soul*. Translated by Gerard Hopkins. Harmondsworth, UK: Penguin Books, 1978.

Note that *Translated by* is spelled out in a bibliography but abbreviated in notes.

EDITIONS OTHER THAN THE FIRST

SN 7. Abrams, *Norton Anthology*, 117–48.

FN 7. M. H. Abrams, ed., *The Norton Anthology of English Literature*, 5th ed. (New York: W. W. Norton, 1987), 117–48.

B Abrams, M. H., ed. *The Norton Anthology of English Literature*. 5th ed. New York: W. W. Norton, 1987.

Particular Volume in a Multivolume Work

SN   8. Kallen, *The 1400s*, 50–55.

FN   8. Stuart A. Kallen, ed., *The 1400s* (San Diego, CA: Greenhaven, 2001), 5:50–55.

B Kallen, Stuart A., ed. *The 1400s*. Vol. 5, *Headlines in History*. San Diego, CA: Greenhaven, 2001.

The full note shown above indicates that all volumes of the Kallen work appeared in 2001. If only Volume 5 had been published in 2001, the note would be formatted as follows:

FN   8. Stuart A. Kallen, ed., *The 1400s*, vol. 5, *Headlines in History* (San Diego, CA: Greenhaven, 2001), 50–55.

Work in an Anthology

SN   9. Morrison, "The Site of Memory," 185–206.

FN   9. Toni Morrison, "The Site of Memory," in *Inventing the Truth: The Art and Craft of Memoir*, ed. William Zinsser (Boston: Houghton Mifflin, 1998), 185–206.

B Morrison, Toni. "The Site of Memory." In *Inventing the Truth: The Art and Craft of Memoir,* edited by William Zinsser, 185–206. Boston: Houghton Mifflin, 1998.

Work in a Series

SN   10. Lecker, David, and Quigley, *Bissoondath*, 29.

FN   10. Robert Lecker, Jack David, and Ellen Quigley, *Bissoondath, Clarke, Kogawa, Mistry, Skvorecky*, Canadian Writers and Their Works 11 (Toronto: ECW, 1996), 29.

B Lecker, Robert, Jack David, and Ellen Quigley. *Bissoondath, Clarke, Kogawa, Mistry, Skvorecky*. Canadian Writers and Their Works 11. Toronto: ECW, 1996.

Dictionary or Encyclopedia

SN   11. *Nelson Canadian Dictionary*, s.v. "saltire."

FN   11. *Nelson Canadian Dictionary of the English Language* (Toronto: ITP Nelson, 1998), s.v. "saltire."

B *Nelson Canadian Dictionary of the English Language*. Toronto: ITP Nelson, 1998.

Well-known reference books are normally cited in notes rather than in bibliographies, with the facts of publication often omitted but with the edition specified. Certain reference works, however, may be listed with publication details, as shown above. For an alphabetically arranged work, cite the item preceded by *s.v.* (for the Latin *sub verbo*, which means "under the word").

PERIODICALS

In the entries below, note that, while specific page references are given in the notes, inclusive pages for the article are given in the bibliographic entries.

ARTICLE IN A JOURNAL

SN   12. Beattie, "Real Place," 11.

FN   12. Ann Beattie, "Real Place, Imagined Life," *Literary Imagination: The Review of the Association of Literary Scholars and Critics* 4, no. 1 (2002): 11.

B Beattie, Ann. "Real Place, Imagined Life." *Literary Imagination: The Review of the Association of Literary Scholars and Critics* 4, no. 1 (2002): 10–16.

Most journal citations include both volume and issue numbers, although the issue number may be omitted if pagination is continuous throughout a volume or when a month or season precedes the year.

ARTICLE IN A MAGAZINE

SN   13. Lazare, "False Testament," 40.

FN   13. Daniel Lazare, "False Testament: Archeology Refutes the Bible Claim to History," *Harper's*, March 2002, 40.

B Lazare, Daniel. "False Testament: Archeology Refutes the Bible Claim to History." *Harper's*, March 2002, 39–47.

ARTICLE IN A NEWSPAPER

SN   14. Reynolds, "UN to Add 'Nazi' Stamp," A2.

FN   14. Matt Reynolds, "UN to Add 'Nazi' Stamp to Auschwitz Camp Site," *Toronto Star*, July 13, 2006, A2.

B Reynolds, Matt. "UN to Add 'Nazi' Stamp to Auschwitz Camp Site." *Toronto Star*, July 13, 2006, A2.

An initial *The* is omitted from a newspaper name. Except for well-known national papers, if the city is not part of the name, it should be added in italics, along with the abbreviated form for the province in parentheses if necessary. For example, *National Post* needs no clarification, but *Daily Gleaner* becomes *Fredericton (NB) Daily Gleaner*.

For unsigned articles, the name of the newspaper stands in place of the author.

ELECTRONIC SOURCES

Many of the rules for citing print sources apply to electronic sources. In addition to the information discussed above, it is important to indicate the medium from which the source was retrieved. A URL is added to the citation to indicate that a source was retrieved from the Internet. If the material is time-sensitive or if the discipline demands it, the retrieval date should be recorded in parentheses as part of the citation.

If a URL has to be broken at the end of a line, do not add a hyphen to denote a line break and do not break a line after a hyphen that is part of the URL. The line break should occur *after* a slash or double slash or before a period, comma, hyphen, tilde (~), or *underscore*.

ONLINE BOOKS

SN   15. Jameson, *The History of Historical Writing*.

FN   15. John Franklin Jameson, *The History of Historical Writing in America* (Boston: Houghton Mifflin, 1891; Electronic Library of Historiography, 1996), accessed July 17, 2006, http://www.eliohs.unifi.it/testi/800/jameson/ jameson.html.

B Jameson, John Franklin. *The History of Historical Writing in America*. Boston: Houghton Mifflin, 1891; Electronic Library of Historiography, 1996. Accessed July 17, 2006. http://www.eliohs.unifi.it/testi/800/jameson/jameson .html.

Wherever possible, include the original facts of publication when citing electronic editions of older works, as in the preceding example.

ONLINE JOURNAL

SN   16. Green, "Poisoned Ears," para. 23.

FN   16. Reina Green. "Poisoned Ears and Parental Advice in *Hamlet*," *Early Modern Literary Studies* 11, no. 3 (2006), para. 23, accessed May 19, 2006, http://www.shu.ac.uk/ emls/11-3/greeham2.htm.

B Green, Reina. "Poisoned Ears and Parental Advice in *Hamlet.*" *Early Modern Literary Studies* 11, no. 3 (2006). Accessed May 19, 2006. http://www.shu.ac.uk/emls/11-3/ greeham2.htm.

Note the descriptive locator, *para. 23,* in the short and full note above, directing readers to a specific location in the article.

WEBSITE

SN 17. Giblin, "Introduction: Diffusion and Other Problems."

FN 17. James Giblin, "Introduction: Diffusion and Other Problems in the History of African States," *Arts and Life in Africa Online,* accessed March 15, 2006, http://www.uiowa .edu/~africart/toc/history/giblistat.html (site discontinued).

B Giblin, James. "Introduction: Diffusion and Other Problems in the History of African States." *Arts and Life in Africa Online*. Accessed March 15, 2006. http://www.uiowa .edu/~africart/toc/history/giblistat.html (site discon- tinued).

If a site ceases to exist, as in the above example, state this parenthetically at the end of the citation.

E-MAIL MESSAGE
References to personal communications such as email mes- sages, letters, and conversations are usually run into the text or given a brief note.

IN TEXT

In an e-mail on July 17, 2006, Damian Collom indicated his displeasure with the new strategic plan.

IN A NOTE

N 18. Damian Collom, e-mail message to author, July 17, 2006.

Personal communications are rarely listed in a bibliography. Be aware, too, that a personal e-mail address may be cited only with the permission of its owner.

N 19. Molly Millar, e-mail to The Design Café mailing list, July 17, 2006, http://lists.graphic-design.net/mailman/listinfo/cafe.

Citations to mailing lists are generally limited to text and notes.

DATABASE

SN 20. Lagapa, "Something from Nothing," 54.

FN 20. Jason Lagapa, "Something from Nothing: Disontological Poetics of Leslie Scalapino," *Contemporary Literature* 47, no. 1 (Spring 2006): 54, accessed July 18, 2006, http://muse.jhu.edu.ezproxy.library.yorku.ca/journals/.

B Lagapa, Jason. "Something from Nothing: Disontological Poetics of Leslie Scalapino." *Contemporary Literature* 47, no. 1 (Spring 2006): 30–61. Accessed July 18, 2006. http://muse.jhu.edu.ezproxy.library.yorku.ca/journals/.

MISCELLANEOUS SOURCES
GOVERNMENT DOCUMENT
Follow these general guidelines for the order of citation elements when citing government documents:

1. Division of government issuing the document
2. Legislative body, department, court, committee, and so forth
3. Subsidiary divisions, regional offices, and so forth
4. Document title
5. Author or editor (if given)
6. Report number or other identifying information
7. Publisher, if different from the issuing body
8. Date
9. Page (if relevant)

SN 21. Treasury Board of Canada, *Canada's Performance*, 8.

FN 21. Treasury Board of Canada, *Canada's Performance: The Government of Canada's Contribution*, 2005, 8.

B Treasury Board of Canada. *Canada's Performance: The Government of Canada's Contribution*. 2005.

The order of these items may vary to suit the subject matter. If the government body issuing the document is not obvious from the context, begin the citation with "Canada," followed by the provincial or territorial legislature.

UNPUBLISHED DISSERTATION

SN   22. Warbey, "The Acquisition of Modal Notions," 90.

FN   22. Margaretta Warbey, "The Acquisition of Modal Notions by Advanced-Level Adult English as a Second Language Learners" (PhD diss., University of Victoria, 1986), 90.

B Warbey, Margaretta. "The Acquisition of Modal Notions by Advanced-Level Adult English as a Second Language Learners." PhD diss., University of Victoria, 1986.

PERSONAL COMMUNICATION
See "E-mail Message" under "Electronic Sources" above.

INTERVIEW

SN   23. Diski, interview.

FN   23. Jenny Diski, interview by Eleanor Wachtel, *Writers & Company*, CBC Radio, July 23, 2006.

B Diski, Jenny. Interview by Eleanor Wachtel. *Writers & Company*. CBC Radio. July 23, 2006.

SOUND RECORDING

SN   24. Gould, *The Goldberg Variations.*

FN   24. Glenn Gould, *The Goldberg Variations,* by Johann Sebastian Bach, Sony Music SMK 52594, compact disc.

B Gould, Glenn. *The Goldberg Variations,* by Johann Sebastian Bach. Sony Music SMK 53594, compact disc.

DVD

SN   25. Young, "When God Made Me."

FN   25. Neil Young, "When God Made Me," *Neil Young: Heart of Gold*, directed by Demme (Hollywood, CA: Paramount, 2005), DVD.

B Young, Neil. "When God Made Me." *Neil Young: Heart of Gold*. Directed by Jonathan Demme. Hollywood, CA: Paramount, 2005. DVD.

Sample Pages

- Title page
- Text page
- Notes page
- Bibliography page

> A page number is not placed on the title page. Note, however, that this page is counted as the first page of the paper.

Historical Criticism and the Work of James Joyce

Carla Thorneloe

Humanities 431

Professor Williams

March 23, 2007

> The title page should include the full title of the paper, your name, the course name, the instructor's name, and the date the paper was submitted.

> NOTE: *The Chicago Manual of Style* does not address the subject of title pages with research papers, so the guidelines on this page are offered to students whose instructors prefer to see title pages with essays.

The page number appears in the upper right-hand corner. Numbering starts on the first page after the title page. Many instructors ask that you use your last name as a header.

The Marxist critic Georg Lukács, in rejecting modernist writers like James Joyce, suggests that their exaggerated concern for formal considerations—"experimental gimmicks" of style and literary technique—reflects a "tendency towards disintegration … [the] loss of artistic unity."[1] Fredric Jameson, a later Marxist critic, also observes fragmentation in literature of the Modernist period, which he identifies as exhibiting reifications. Jameson defines reification as

> a disease of that mapping function whereby the individual subject projects and models his or her own insertion into the collectivity…. The reification of late capitalism—the transformation of relations into an appearance of relationships between things—renders society opaque; it is the lived source of mystification on which ideology is based and by which domination and exploitation are legitimized.[2]

With the market exchange-value economy, people are commodified—they become depersonalized, reduced to mere things. We see evidence of this in *Ulysses* when Buck Mulligan remarks, "Redheaded women buck like goats," and when, through Father Conmee's intelligence, we learn "a tiny yawn opened the mouth of the wife of the gentleman with the glasses."[3] In both instances people are described in terms of things. Jameson suggests that capitalism is

The note number signals an acknowledgment. The number 2 corresponds to the second entry in the "Notes" section of the paper.

The endnotes section continues the pagination of the paper.

Indent the first line of the entry 1.25 cm (0.5 in.). Each subsequent line should be flush with the left margin.

Centre the title "Notes" and set it 2.5 cm (1 in.) from the top of the page.

Notes

1. Georg Lukács, *Realism in Our Time* (New York: Harper and Row, 1964), 37.

2. Fredric Jameson, "Reflections in Conclusion," *Aesthetics and Politics*, ed. Ronald Taylor (London: New Left Books, 1977), 212.

3. James Joyce, *Ulysses* (Harmondsworth, UK: Penguin Books, 1985), 19, 183.

Numbers do not appear in superscript.

4. Georg Lukács, *The Meaning of Contemporary Realism* (London: Merlin Press, 1979), 21.

5. Arthur Power, *Conversations with James Joyce*, ed. Clive Hart (Chicago: Univ. of Chicago Press, 1974), 95.

6. Richard Ellmann, *James Joyce* (Oxford: Oxford Univ. Press, 1959), 459.

7. Lukács, *Meaning of Contemporary Realism*, 39.

This note makes reference to a book that was cited earlier, so the entry can be shortened. The title is needed because the writer of the paper also cited other works by this author.

8. Hugh Kenner, *Dublin's Joyce* (Bloomington: Indiana Univ. Press, 1956), 60.

Authors' names appear with the first name first.

9. William C. Dowling, *Jameson, Altusser, Marx: An Introduction to the Political Unconscious* (Ithaca, NY: Cornell Univ. Press, 1984), 26.

10. Terry Eagleton, *Marxism and Literary Criticism* (London: Methuen, 1976), 27.

11. Marilyn French, "Joyce and Language," *James Joyce Quarterly* 19, no. 3 (1982): 240.

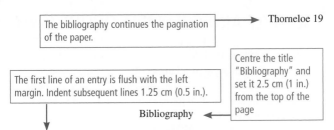

The bibliography continues the pagination of the paper.

The first line of an entry is flush with the left margin. Indent subsequent lines 1.25 cm (0.5 in.).

Centre the title "Bibliography" and set it 2.5 cm (1 in.) from the top of the page

Bibliography

Dowling, William C. *Jameson, Altusser, Marx: An Introduction to the Political Unconscious*. Ithaca, NY: Cornell Univ. Press, 1984.

Eagleton, Terry. *Marxism and Literary Criticism*. London: Methuen, 1976.

Ellmann, Richard. *James Joyce*. Oxford: Oxford Univ. Press, 1959.

French, Marilyn. "Joyce and Language." *James Joyce Quarterly* 19, no. 3 (1982): 227–50.

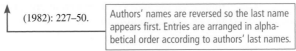

Authors' names are reversed so the last name appears first. Entries are arranged in alphabetical order according to authors' last names.

Gennette, Gerard. *Narrative Discourse: An Essay in Method*. Ithaca, NY: Cornell Univ. Press, 1972.

Jameson, Fredric. "Reflections in Conclusion." *Aesthetics and Politics*. Edited by Ronald Taylor, 196–213. London: New Left Books, 1977.

Joyce, James. *Ulysses*. Harmondsworth, UK: Penguin Books, 1985.

Kenner, Hugh. *Dublin's Joyce*. Bloomington: Indiana Univ. Press, 1956.

Lukács, Georg. *Realism in Our Time*. New York: Harper and Row, 1964.

___. *The Meaning of Contemporary Realism*. London: Merlin Press, 1979.

When more than one work by an author is cited, you may use a 3-em dash in place of the author's name for entries after the first. Arrange such entries in alphabetical order.

Power, Arthur. *Conversations with James Joyce*. Edited by Clive Hart. Chicago: Univ. of Chicago Press, 1974.

Williams, Raymond. *Marxism and Literature*. Oxford: Oxford Univ. Press, 1977.

CSE STYLE AND COLUMBIA ONLINE STYLE

The Council of Science Editors (CSE) is the recognized authority on documentation style in all areas of science and related fields. Documentation guidelines presented in *Scientific Style and Format: The CSE Manual for Authors, Editors, and Publishers* (7th ed., 2006) are outlined below.

Columbia Online Style (COS) has variations for humanities and scientific disciplines and can be useful for citing electronic sources no matter which specific style of documentation you are required to use.

CSE Style of Documentation

DOCUMENTATION STYLES

The *CSE Manual* outlines three styles of documentation: name-year, citation-sequence, and citation-name.

NAME-YEAR
This system is very similar to APA style. Sources are identified in the text in parenthetical name-year references with complete bibliographical information given at the end of the paper in a reference list organized alphabetically by author surname. As the following examples illustrate, CSE style emphasizes simplicity, avoiding effects such as italics and reducing punctuation to a minimum.

> *In-Text Reference*
> Dietary soy intake in man is proposed to provide cardiovascular protection, but it is not established whether this property is attributable to the soy protein per se or to associated dietary isoflavones (Douglas et al. 2006).

> *End Reference*
> Douglas G, Armitage JA, Taylor PD, Lawson JR, Mann GE, Poston L. 2006. Cardiovascular consequences of life-long exposure to dietary isoflavones in the rat. J Physiol. 571(2):477–487.

In CSE style, names are given for up to 10 authors and *et al.* used only after the 10th. Notice that journal names are abbreviated and use of spaces and punctuation is minimal.

CITATION-SEQUENCE
In this system, superscript numbers in the text correspond to numbered references in a list at the end of the document. References are numbered in the order in which they appear

within the text, with the number placed immediately after the reference in the text and before any punctuation. If the sentence uses the authority's name, the number is inserted after the name. If a single reference points to more than one source, numbers are given in a series, with commas and no spaces separating discontinuous numbers and a hyphen inserted to show more than two inclusive source numbers.

... the incidence of T cells was seen[2,9,13–17,22,23] to decrease ...

Once a source has been assigned a number, it is referred to by that number throughout.

In the reference list, entries are ordered in the sequence in which they first appear in the text, with numbers placed on the line followed by a period and a space. For example, if the first reference in the text is to a work by Zeleny, number 1 in the reference list at the end of the paper will be Zeleny.

In-Text Reference

Savage-Rumbaugh and Lewin's[1] work on Kanzi describes a chimpanzee who understands a good deal of spoken English, and the text expands our notions of what constitutes animal intelligence. McCarthy and Masson[2] wrote a book that not only touched on a subject not much examined before—animals' emotions—but became a popular nonfiction work as well.

End Reference

1. Savage-Rumbaugh ES, Lewin R. The ape at the brink of the human mind. New York: Wiley; 1994. 299 p.

2. McCarthy S, Masson JM. When elephants weep: the emotional lives of animals. New York: Delacorte; 1995. 291 p.

Note that the last element of these entries indicates the total number of pages in a book. This is an optional component of a book reference, but it can be useful for the reader.

CITATION-NAME

In this system, the list of end references is compiled alphabetically by author surname. The references are then numbered in that sequence, with Aaba number 1, Backnell number 2, and so on. These numbers are used for in-text references regardless of the sequence in which they appear in the text. If Mobbitt is number 38 in the reference list, the in-text reference is number 38, and the same number is used for subsequent in-text references.

When several in-text references occur at the same point, place their corresponding reference list numbers in numeric order. In-text reference numbers not in a continuous sequence are separated by commas with no spaces. For more than two numbers in a continuous sequence, connect the first and last by a hyphen.

> ... in several research projects[2,7–11,16,25] that had shown ...

END REFERENCES

PAGE LAYOUT
Begin your reference list on a separate page with the centred title *References* or *Cited References* at the top. Single-space with a blank line between entries. Use a flush-left style for entries (no hanging indent).

SEQUENCE OF REFERENCES
Give the reference number in regular type followed by a period and a space. For the name-year system, place references in alphabetical order by author. For citation-sequence, list and number end references in the order in which they are cited in the text. For citation-name, place references in alphabetical order by author and then number the in-text references in the same sequence.

EXAMPLES OF CSE STYLE
The following examples illustrate the correct formatting for end references as they would occur in either the citation-sequence or citation-name system. For the name–year system, the date is moved up to follow the author name.

Book with One Author
1. Hawking SW. 2001. The universe in a nutshell. New York: Bantam. 216 p.

Book with More Than One Author
2. McCarthy S, Masson JM. 1995. When elephants weep: the emotional lives of animals. New York: Delacorte. 291 p.

Edited Book
3. Bowling AT, Ruvinsky A, editors. 2000. The genetics of the horse. New York: Oxford University Press. p. 527.

Chapter from an Edited Book
4. Polanyi JC. 1992. The transition state. In: Zewail AH, editor. The chemical bond: structure and dynamics. Boston: Academic Press. p. 201–227.

EDITION OTHER THAN THE FIRST
   5. Lyon MF, Searle AG, editors. 2000. Genetic variants and
      strains of the laboratory mouse. 3rd ed. New York: Oxford
      University Press. 896 p.

JOURNAL ARTICLE WITH VOLUME AND ISSUE NUMBERS
   6. Reimann N, Barnitzeke S, Nolte I, Bullerdick J. 1999.
      Working with canine chromosomes: current recommenda-
      tions for karyotype description. J Hered. 90(1):31–34.

JOURNAL ARTICLE WITH DISCONTINUOUS PAGINATION
   7. Crews D, Gartska WR. 1981. The ecological physiology of
      the garter snake. Sci Am. 245:158–164,166–168.

NEWSPAPER ARTICLE
   8. Vincent D. 1st West Nile case reported. Toronto Star. 2006
      Aug 20; Sect. A3 (col. 5).

WEBSITE
   9. Canadian Science Writers' Association [homepage on the
      Internet]. 2006. Toronto (ON): Canadian Science Writers'
      Association; [updated 2006 Aug 15; cited 2006 Aug 22].
      Available from: http://www.sciencewriters.ca/index.html

ONLINE BOOK
   10. Farabee MJ. The online biology book [Internet]. 2001.
       Avondale (AZ): Estrella Mountain Community College;
       [updated 2001 Sep 17; cited 2006 Aug 22]. Available from:
       http://www.emc.maricopa.edu/faculty/farabee/BIOBK/
       BioBookTOC.html

ONLINE ARTICLE
   11. Brown VW. Neurofeedback and Lyme's disease: a clinical
       application of the five phase model of CNS functional
       transformation and integration. JNT [Internet]. 1995 Fall
       [cited 2006 Aug 22]; 1(2):[about 32 screens]. Available from:
       http://www.snr-jnt.org/journalnt/jnt(1-2)6.html

ONLINE DATABASE
   12. Alcohol and Alcohol Problems Science Database (ETOH)
       [Internet]. 1972–2003. Bethesda (MD): National Institute on
       Alcohol Abuse and Alcoholism. [cited 2006 Aug 22].
       Available from: http://etoh.niaaa.nih.gov/Archive.htm

Columbia Online Style of Documentation

The following material is based on Janice R. Walker and Todd
Taylor's *The Columbia Guide to Online Style*, 2nd ed. (New York:
Columbia University Press, 2006).

Citing information from online sources can be difficult. For one thing, sites often move or disappear; for another, websites often fail to supply the detailed information necessary to cite them properly. To date, no single standard exists for documenting online sources, but COS offers practical guidelines for citing electronic sources in both the humanities and the sciences.

HUMANITIES STYLE

COS uses a humanities style based on MLA criteria but modified for online sources. As with other styles, citations include a note in the text and a matching entry in a list of works cited that gives complete bibliographic information.

IN-TEXT REFERENCES

Although page numbers are usually given in the case of print documents, they rarely appear within an electronic document or file. In-text references therefore usually include only the author's last name, either in the body of the text or in parentheses next to quoted or paraphrased material:

> Cohen states that North American audiences responded negatively.

> North American audiences responded negatively (Cohen).

If no author is named, cite the name of the corporation or organization:

> In the 2001 Census, it was found that both divorce and marriage were on the rise (Statistics Canada).

When no author or organization is listed, use the document title or a shortened version of the title:

> ("Jazz Beat")

> (*CBC.ca*)

For citations with no author or title, use the file name:

> (18165.html)

For multiple works by the same author, include the author's last name followed by a comma and a shortened version of the title. This information can be given either in a parenthetical note or in the text.

BIBLIOGRAPHIC ENTRIES

The list of works cited should begin on a separate page and should be double-spaced throughout. When citing electronic sources, attempt to include in bibliographic citations as many of the following key information elements as you can:

1. **Author's last name**, followed by a comma and the first name and initial(s) (if known).
2. **Title of document.** For untitled files, give a designation (for example, *Home Page*), with no quotation marks or italics. End with a period.
3. **Title of complete work.** Capitalize the first word and all major words and set in italics. End with a period.
4. **Version or edition**, if applicable, followed by a period.
5. **Date of publication or last revision**, if available, in international date format (day, month, year), followed by a period.
6. **Protocol and address**, or name of database (in italics) and publisher.
7. **Access path**, directories, keywords, or file numbers, if applicable, in parentheses.
8. **Date of access**, in parentheses, in day-month-year format, followed by a period.

Following are some examples of citations for electronic sources in the humanities. Other examples can be found in the COS manual.

WEBPAGE

Munroe, Randall. Brand Identity. xkcd.com 21 Dec. 2011.

http://www.xkcd.com/993/ 16 Jan. 2012).

WEBSITE

National Association of Photoshop Professionals. NAPP. 2006.

http://www.photoshopuser.com (6 Nov. 2006).

FULL-TEXT ARTICLE FROM LIBRARY DATABASE

Goldie, Terry. "The Canadian Homosexual." *Journal of*

Canadian Studies, 33.4 (Winter 1998/1999): 132–143.

Research Library. ProQuest. ISSN 00219495 (8 Nov.

2006).

ABSTRACT FROM LIBRARY DATABASE

Cohen, Mark. Abstract. "Just Judgment: Censorship of and in

Canadian Literature." Diss. McGill University, 1999.

ProQuest Dissertations and Theses. ProQuest. AAT

NQ50133 (8 Nov. 2006).

ONLINE REFERENCE WORK

"Philistine." *Merriam-Webster OnlineDictionary. Merriam-*

Webster OnLine. 2006. http://www.m-w.com/dictionary/

Philistine (6 Nov. 2006).

MAILING LIST

Long, Tom. "Re: Certification." 6 Nov. 2006. *Editors'*

*Association of Canada members' discussion lis*t. eac-acr

-l@list.web.net (6 Nov. 2006).

SCIENTIFIC STYLE

For scientific sources, COS style is designed to complement
APA guidelines for citing print sources while providing more
complete suggestions for citing electronic sources. As with
other styles, citations include a note in the text and a matching
entry in the list of references, which gives complete bibliographic information.

IN-TEXT REFERENCES

Since most electronic sources are not paginated, in-text references include only the author's last name followed by a
comma and the year of publication:

The glycerol produced during transesterification contains a
very high percentage of excess methanol (Kemp, 2006).

Subsequent references may omit the date, giving only the author's name.

If there is no publication date, use the date of access (day-month-year):

> There is no concrete evidence to suggest that the drug is effective in controlling performance anxiety (Millar, 8 Nov. 2006).

If the author's name is given in the text, include the date in parentheses immediately after the author's name:

> Fenton (2006) claims that many events are either silent or clinically unrecognized.

Two or more references in the same note are separated with a semicolon:

> (Peters & Collom, 2005; Stendall, 2006)

If no author is given, use the document or webpage title and the date:

> ("Quirks & Quarks," 2006) (CBC.ca, 2006)

BIBLIOGRAPHIC ENTRIES

The list of works cited should begin on a separate page and should be double-spaced throughout. When citing electronic sources, attempt to include in bibliographic citations as many of the following key information elements as you can:

1. **Author's last name and initial(s)**, or the author's e-mail, login name, or alias. Use a comma after the last name and end with a period.
2. **Date of document,** in parentheses, followed by a period.
3. **Title of document**, capitalizing only the first word, any proper nouns, and the first word following a colon, if applicable. End with a period.
4. **Title of complete work**, in italics, capitalizing only the first word and any proper nouns. End with a period.
5. **Edition or revision**, if applicable, enclosed in parentheses and followed by a period.
6. **Protocol and address**, or name of database (in italics) and database publisher.
7. **Access path**, or directories or document or file number, in parentheses.
8. **Date of access**, in parentheses, followed by a period.

Following are some examples of citations for electronic sources in the sciences. Other examples can be found in the COS manual.

WEBPAGE

Nobel Foundation. (2006). The Nobel Prize in Chemistry.

Nobelprize.org. http://nobelprize.org/nobel_prizes/

chemistry (8 Nov. 2006).

WEBSITE

National Biodiesel Board. (2006). *Biodiesel*. http://www.biod-

iesel.org (8 Nov. 2006).

FULL-TEXT ARTICLE FROM LIBRARY DATABASE

Maviglia, M.A. (2006). Alcohol and drug abuse intervention in

the emergency department. *Psychiatric Times*, *23*(1),

40. *ProQuest Nursing & Allied Health*. ProQuest. (ISSN

08932905) (8 Nov. 2006).

ABSTRACT FROM LIBRARY DATABASE

Kuhlen, M. (2006). Adventures in numerical cosmology

[Abstract]. *ProQuest Dissertations and Theses*.

ProQuest. (9780542705502) (8 Nov. 2006).

ONLINE REFERENCE WORK

Maquiladrora. (2006). In *Encyclopaedia Britannica online*.

http://www.britannica.com/EBchecked/topic/363663/

maquiladora (12 Nov. 2011).

MAILING LIST

Fennel, R. (2006, November 8). Re: Editing science texts.

Editors' Association of Canada members' discussion list.

eac-acr-l@list.web.net (8 Nov. 2006).

IEEE STYLE OF DOCUMENTATION

The IEEE (Institute of Electrical and Electronic Engineers) method of documentation is most commonly used in engineering courses. You will notice the main features that separate IEEE from MLA format are the author's name (first name before last name), the use of commas instead of periods to separate items in most cases, and the order in which the references appear in the *References* list.

References

Instead of parenthetical in-text citations, when you are following the IEEE documentation style, you must insert within the text a number in square brackets that points to the reference in the list at the end of the document. Compile a References list on a separate page at the end of your paper and arrange the references numerically. If you use the same reference twice, you should use the same number as you did the first time.

FORMAT OF A REFERENCES LIST

TITLE AND PLACEMENT
Start the list of works cited on a new page at the end of your research paper. Title it *References* and centre the title at the top of the page. The title *References* allows you to include books and articles, as well as films, recordings, websites, television programs, and other non-print sources.

PAGINATION
Continue the page numbering of the text throughout the *References* list; for example, if the last page of your research paper is 15, the first page of references would be 16. Position page numbers in the upper right-hand corner.

SPACING
Single-space entries and between entries.

ARRANGEMENT OF ENTRIES
Arrange entries in the *References* list by the order in which they appear in the document numerically. Examples of references entries are shown below.

BOOKS

The publication details for a book are found on the **title page** and on the reverse side of the title page, which is known as the **copyright page**. A very few books have publication information at the back of the book. When writing an entry, use information from the source itself as opposed to information from a bibliography or library catalogue. This will reduce the chance of errors in your entry.

AUTHOR'S NAME
Put the author's first (or more) initial(s), followed by a period and a space, and then the last name. Put a comma after the complete name. If there are three or more authors, write the first author's name, followed by *et al.*

TITLE OF CHAPTER IN BOOK
Put the title of the chapter in quotation marks, with a comma before the closing quotation.

BOOK TITLE
Provide the full name of the book, including any subtitles. The entire title, but not the period following it, should be italicized. Capitalize important words within the title. If there is a subtitle, separate it from the main title with a colon and one space. Always capitalize the first and last words in any subtitle. Precede the title with the word *in* if you include the title of a chapter of the book. End the title with a comma and leave one space before the publication information, plus the page range if the source is a chapter.

EDITION
State the ordinal number (for example, 1st, 2nd, 3rd), followed by the abbreviation *ed.*, meaning edition, and a space.

PUBLICATION INFORMATION

PLACE OF PUBLICATION: If several cities are listed on the title or copyright pages, use only the first. Place a colon and one space between the city of publication and the name of the publisher. For cities outside the United States that may be unfamiliar or ambiguous, add a comma and the province or country in abbreviated form. For example, if London, Ontario, is meant rather than London, England, write *London, ON*. For a foreign city, you may substitute the English name or add a translation in brackets.

PUBLISHER: You do not need to use the complete name of the publisher; simply give enough information to enable your reader to find the source easily. Omit any articles (*A, An, The*), common abbreviations (*Inc., Co.,* and *Ltd.*), and descriptive words (*Books, House, Press,* and *Publishers*). However, for university presses always include the abbreviation *Univ.* (e.g., *Oxford Univ. Press* or *Univ. of Chicago Press*) because the university itself may publish independently of its press. If the publishing company includes the name of one person, cite the surname alone (*Norton* rather than *W. W. Norton*). Place a comma between the name of the publisher and the year of publication.

YEAR OF PUBLICATION: If no date appears on the title page, use the latest copyright date. Place a comma between the year of publication and chapter/section/page numbers.

SINGLE AUTHOR

[1] J.L. Blackburn, *Protective Relaying*. New York: Dekker, 1997.

TWO OR THREE AUTHORS
Give the authors' names in the same order as they appear on the title page, which may not be in alphabetical order.

[2] E. M. Mikhail, J.S. Bethel, and C.J. McGlone, *Introduction to Modern Photogrammetry*. New York: John Wiley and Sons, 2001.

EDITOR(S)

[3] B. A. Osif, Ed., *Using the Engineering Literature*. London: Routledge, 2006.

TRANSLATION

[4] J. Bertin, *Semiology of Graphics*, W.J. Berg, Trans. Madison, WI: Univ. of Wisconsin Press, 1983.

CORPORATE AUTHOR

[5] Westinghouse Electric Corporation, *Westinghouse Relay Manual: A New Silent Sentinels Publication*. Newark, NJ: Westinghouse Electric Corporation, 1972.

ENCYCLOPEDIA, DICTIONARY, OR OTHER REFERENCE WORK

[6] O. B. R. Strimpel, "Computer graphics," in *McGraw-Hill Encyclopedia of Science and Technology*, 8th ed., Vol. 4. New York: McGraw-Hill, 1997, pp. 279–283.

HANDBOOK

[7] *Product Safety Label Handbook: Danger, Warning, Caution*. Westinghouse Electric Corporation, Cranberry Township, PA, 1981.

REPORT

[8] J. H. Connell, "A colony architecture for an artificial creature," MIT AI Lab Technical Report, Cambridge, MA, Rep. 1151, June 1989.

ARTICLES

Give the author name followed by a comma, the name of the article in quotation marks with a comma inside, and the name of the magazine, italicized and followed by the series number, volume number, page numbers, and month and year. With the exception of May, June, and July, abbreviate the months.

ARTICLE IN A MONTHLY MAGAZINE

[9] I. E. Sutherland, R. F. Sproull, and R. A. Schumaker, "A characterization of 10 hidden-surface algorithms," *ACM Comp. Sur.,* pp. 1–55, Mar. 1974.

ARTICLE IN ANOTHER LANGUAGE

[10] E. P. Wigner, "On a modification of the Rayleigh–Schrodinger perturbation theory," (in German), *Math. Naturwiss. Anz. Ungar. Akad. Wiss.*, vol. 53, p. 475, 1935.

TRANSLATED ARTICLE

[11] Ye. V. Lavrova, "Geographic distribution of ionospheric disturbances in the F2 layer," Tr. *IZMIRAN*, vol. 19, no. 29, pp. 31–43, 1961 (Transl.: E. R. Hope, Directorate of Scientific Information Services, Defence Research Board of Canada, Rep. T384R, Apr. 1963).

UNPUBLISHED PAPER OR REPORT

[12] K. Riley, "Language theory: Applications versus practice," presented at the Conference of the Modern Language Association, Boston, MA, 1990.

ARTICLE IN AN ENCYCLOPEDIA

[13] O. B. R. Strimpel, "Computer graphics," in *McGraw-Hill Encyclopedia of Science and Technology*, 8th ed., Vol. 4. New York: McGraw-Hill, 1997, pp. 279–283.

ELECTRONIC SOURCES

E-BOOK

[14] D. Horowitz. *End of Time*. New York: Encounter Books, 2005. [E-book] Available: ebrary, http://site.ebrary.com/lib/sait/Doc?id=10080005. [Accessed: Oct. 8, 2008].

CHAPTER FROM AN E-BOOK

[15] M. A. Shotton, "Computing activities: The nature of the phenomenon," in *Computer Addiction? A Study of Computer Dependency*. London: Taylor and Francis, 1989, 61–82. [E-book]. Available: GoogleBooks.

ARTICLE FROM AN ELECTRONIC ENCYCLOPEDIA

[15] G. Graham, "Behaviourism," in *The Stanford encyclopedia of philosophy*, E. N. Zalta, Ed. [E-Book]. Available: http://plato.stanford.edu/entries/behaviourism.

JOURNAL ARTICLE FROM A FULL TEXT DATABASE

[16] H. Ayasso and A. Mohammad-Djafari, "Joint NDT image restoration and segmentation using Gauss–Markov–Potts prior models and variational Bayesian computation," *IEEE Transactions on Image Processing*, vol. 19, no. 9, pp. 2265–2277, 2010. [Online]. Available: IEEE Xplore, http://www.ieee.org. [Accessed Sept. 10, 2010].

JOURNAL ARTICLE FROM THE INTERNET

[17] R. M. Sharkey and D. M. Goldenberg, "Targeted therapy of cancer: new prospects for antibodies and immunocon-jugates," *CA: Cancer Journal for Clinicians*, vol. 56, no. 4, pp. 226–243, Jul./Aug. 2006. [Online]. Available: http://caonline.amcancersoc.org/cgi/content/full/56/4/226. [Accessed Oct. 18, 2006].

ELECTRONIC DOCUMENT

[18] T. Land, "Web extension to American Psychological Association style (WEAPAS)," Mar. 31, 1996 (Rev.1.2.4) [Online]. Available: http://www.nyu.edu/pages/psychology/WEAPAS/. [Accessed Sept. 14, 1996].

GOVERNMENT PUBLICATION

[19] J. Martel, "Analysis of the waste management practices at Bosnia and Kosovo base camps," US Army Corps of Engineers, Hanover, NH, Tech. Rep. ERDC/CRRELTR-03-6, April 2003.

INTERNET SITE

[20] R. McKie, "Hope rises for new cancer treatment after tests with electromagnetism," *guardian.co.uk*, para. 3, Jan. 7,

2012. Available: http://www.guardian.co.uk/science/2012/
jan/08/electromagnetic-fields-could-stop-cancer. [Accessed:
Jan. 9, 2012].

AUDIO-VISUAL MATERIALS

DVD

[21] B. Cox, Presenter, J. Renouf, Producer, *Wonders of the
Universe* [DVD]. London, UK: BBC, 2011.

RADIO PROGRAM

[22] J. Mayers, Producer. "Episode 5," *Dear Professor Hawking*,
Jan. 6, 2012 [Radio broadcast]. London, UK: BBC Radio 4.

SOUND RECORDING

[23] P. Magrs, Writer, and T. Baker, Presenter, *Doctor Who:
Demon Quest* [Sound recording]. Bath, UK: BBC
Audiobooks, 2011.

TELEVISION PROGRAM

[24] D. Attenborough, Writer and Presenter, "On Thin Ice."
Frozen Planet, Dec. 7, 2011 [Television broadcast]. London,
UK: BBC Television.

VIDEO RECORDING

[25] T. Friedman, Executive Producer, "Matters of life and
death," *A Science Odyssey* [Videorecording]. Arlington,
VA: PBS, 1998.

CONFERENCE PAPERS

CONFERENCE PAPER

[25] C. P. Behrenbruch et al., "MRI-Mammography 2D/3D Data
Fusion for Breast Pathology Assessment" presented at the
Third Annual Conference on Medical Image Computing
and Computer-Assisted Intervention—MICCAI 2000, Oct.
11–14, 2000, pp. 307–316.

CONFERENCE PAPER FROM THE INTERNET

[25] K. Kosuge, "Human-robot interaction: What we learned
from robot helpers and dance partner robots," in *The 17th
IEEE International Symposium on Robot and Human
Interactive Communication*, 2008. Aug. 1-3, 2008, Munich,

Germany. Available: IEEE Xplore, http://www.ieee
.org. [Accessed: Jan. 9, 2012].

UNPUBLISHED CONFERENCE PAPER

[26] H. A. Nimr, "Defuzzification of the outputs of fuzzy con-
trollers," presented at 5th International Conference on
Fuzzy Systems, 1996, Cairo, Egypt. 1996.

CONFERENCE PROCEEDINGS

[27] D. B. Payne and J. R. Stern, "Wavelength-switched pas-
sively coupled single-mode optical network," in *Proc.
IOOC-ECOC*, 1985, pp. 585–590.

NEWSPAPER ARTICLES

NEWSPAPER ARTICLE

[28] J. Vasagar, "Britain's computer science courses failing to
give workers digital skills," *The Guardian*, p. 1, Jan 10,
2012.

NEWSPAPER ARTICLE FROM THE INTERNET

[29] P. J. Hilts, "In forecasting their emotions, most people
flunk out," *The New York Times*, Feb. 6, 1999. [Online].
Available: http://www.nytimes.com. [Accessed: Feb. 19,
2000].

NEWSPAPER ARTICLE FROM A FULL TEXT DATABASE

[30] J. Riley, "Call for new look at skilled migrants," *The
Australian*, p. 35, May 31, 2005. [Online]. Available:
Factiva, http://global.factiva.com. [Accessed May 31, 2005].

PODCASTS

PODCAST

[31] D. Van Nuys, Producer, "The anatomy of a lobotomist
[Show 84]," *Shrink Rap Radio*, 2007. [Podcast]. Available:
http://www.shrinkrapradio.com/. [Accessed April 11, 2007].

PODCAST RADIO PROGRAM

[32] N. Swan, Presenter, and B. Seega, Producer, "Health effects
of exercise," *ABC Radio National*, November 12, 2007,
[Podcast radio program]. Sydney, Australia: ABC News
Radio. Available: http://www.abc.net.au/rn/healthreport/
stories/2007/2085642.htm. [Accessed Oct. 14, 2008].

PODCAST TELEVISION PROGRAM

[33] W. Brown and K. Brodie, Presenters, and P. George, Producer, "From Lake Baikal to the Halfway Mark, Yekaterinburg," *Peking to Paris: Episode 3*, Jun. 4, 2007. Sydney: ABC Television. [Podcast television program]. Available: http://www.abc.net.au/tv/pekingtoparis/podcast/pekingtoparis.xml. [Accessed Feb. 4, 2008].

THESES

If the location of the thesis is stated in the name of the university (for example, University of Calgary), stating the city and state/province again in the location is not necessary.

UNPUBLISHED PAPER

[34] S. Mack, "Desperate optimism," unpublished.

UNPUBLISHED THESIS

[35] J. O. Williams, "Narrow-band analyzer," Ph.D. dissertation, Dept. Elect. Eng., Harvard Univ., Cambridge, MA, 1993.

THESIS FROM A FULL TEXT DATABASE

[36] F. Sudweeks, *Development and Leadership in Computer-Mediated Collaborative Groups*. Ph.D. dissertation [Online]. Murdoch, WA: Murdoch Univ., 2007. Available: http://researchrepository.murdoch.edu.au/352/1/01Front.pdf.

GLOSSARY OF USAGE
glossary of usage

GLOSSARY OF USAGE

How Can the Glossary of Usage Help You?

The glossary will help you to make correct word choices in both your formal and informal writing and speaking. It will do this by providing the following information:

- definitions of words
- sample sentences using words correctly in context
- preferred formal usage for academic writing
- commonly confused words (*explicit, implicit*)
- non-standard vocabulary (*anyways*)
- colloquialisms (*flunk*)
- jargon (*finalize*)
- non-inclusive language (*mankind*)
- redundancies (*and etc.*)
- parts of speech for many words
- cross-references to other relevant handbook sections
- homophones (*night, knight*)
- common abbreviations
- prefixes (*dis-*) and suffixes (*-ness*)

a, an. Use *a* before a word that begins with a consonant sound, even if the word begins with a vowel: *a computer, a desk, a unique individual, a university.* Use *an* before a word that begins with a vowel sound, even if the word begins with a consonant: *an iguana, an oak, an hour, an honour.* Words beginning with the letter *h* often present problems. Generally, if the initial *h* sound is hard, use *a*: *a hot dog, a heart attack.* However, if the initial *h* is silent, use *an*: *an honest mistake.* If the *h* is pronounced, Canadian writers generally use *a* with the word: *a history, a hotel.*

accept, except. *Accept* is a verb meaning "to receive" or "take to (oneself)." *He accepted the lottery prize. Except* is very rarely a verb; usually, it is a preposition meaning "to exclude." *Everyone except Jerome received a penalty.*

adapt, adopt. *Adapt* means to "adjust oneself to" or "make suitable," and it is followed by the preposition *to*. *The lizard will adapt to its surroundings.* The word *adapt* can also mean "revise," in which case it is used with the preposition *for* or *from*. *They will adapt the novel for the silver screen. Adopt* means "to take or use as one's own." *They plan to adopt the idea for their computer game.*

adverse, averse. *Adverse* means "unfavourable." *Smoking has an adverse effect on your health. Averse* means "opposed" or "having an active distaste"; it can also mean "reluctant," in which case it is followed by the preposition *to*. *She was averse to fighting of any kind.*

advice, advise. *Advice* is a noun that means "an opinion about what should be done." *Take my advice and sell while you can. Advise* is a verb that means "to offer advice." *The high-priced lawyer will advise us on what course of action to take.*

affect, effect. *Affect* is a verb that most commonly means "to influence." *Water pollution affects the health of fish. Effect* is often a noun meaning "result." *The artist flicked paint on the canvas but could not achieve the effect he wanted. Effect* can also be used as a verb meaning "to bring about or execute." *The cost-cutting moves will effect a turnaround for the business.*

aggravate, irritate. *Aggravate* is a verb that means "to make worse or more severe." *The boy's cold was aggravated by the dry air. Irritate*, a verb, means "to make impatient or angry." Note that *aggravate* is often used colloquially to mean *irritate*. Do not substitute *aggravate* for *irritate* in formal writing. *His constant complaining irritated* [not *aggravated*] *me.*

agree to, agree with. *Agree to* means "to consent to." *The two sides will agree to the proposal. Agree with* means "to be in accord with." *The witness's version of events agrees with theirs.*

ain't. *Ain't* means "am not," "are not," or "is not." It is non-standard English and should not be used in formal writing.

all ready, already. *All ready* means "completely prepared." *The sprinter is all ready for the starter's gun. Already* is an adverb that means "before this time; previously; even now." *They have already seen* The Lion King.

all right, alright. *All right* is always written as two words. *Alright* is non-standard English for *all right* and should not be used in formal writing. *It's all right* [not *alright*] *to eat dinner if Desmond is late.*

all together, altogether. See *altogether, all together.*

allude, elude. *Allude* means "to refer to indirectly or casually." Do not use it to mean "to refer to directly." *In his presentation, Freud specifically referred to* [not *alluded to*] *the importance of the subconscious. Elude* means "to evade or escape from, usually with some daring or skill," or "to escape the understanding or grasp of." *I eluded my pursuers, but why they were chasing me eluded me.*

allusion, illusion, delusion. *Allusion* is an "implied or indirect reference." *The prosecuting attorney made an allusion to her criminal past.* The word *illusion* means "an appearance or feeling that misleads because it is not real." *When the bus beside ours backed up, it created the illusion that we were moving.* This should be distinguished from *delusion*, which means "a false and often harmful belief about something that does not exist." *The paranoid reporter had the delusion that every e-mail contained a virus.*

alot, a lot. *A lot* is always written as two words. *We have not had a lot of snow this winter.* Avoid using *a lot* in formal writing.

altogether, all together. *Altogether* means "completely, entirely." *Altogether there were eight novels assigned for the course.* The phrase *all together* means "together in a group." *We found the litter of puppies all together in the garage.*

a.m., p.m. Use these abbreviations only with specific times, when numerals are provided: *10 a.m.* or *1 p.m.* Do not use the abbreviations as substitutes for *morning, afternoon,* or *evening. The mother had to get up early in the morning* [not *the a.m.*] *to take her daughter to the hockey game.*

among, between. See *between, among.*

amoral, immoral. *Amoral* means "not having any morals; neither moral nor immoral." *The cabinet adopted an amoral perspective when they considered tax cuts.* The word *immoral* means "morally wrong or wicked." *It is immoral to steal food from the food bank.*

amount, number. *Amount* is used to refer to things in bulk or mass. These things cannot be counted. *A large amount of litter can be found along the highway. Number* is used to refer to things that can be counted. *He gobbled down a number of bedtime snacks every evening.*

an, a. See *a, an.*

and etc. *etc.* (*et cetera*) means "and so forth." Do not use *and etc.* because it is redundant. See also *etc.*

and/or. *And/or* is sometimes used to indicate three possibilities: one, or the other, or both. It is occasionally acceptable in business, technical, or legal writing. Avoid this awkward construction when writing for the humanities.

ante-, anti-. *Ante-* is a prefix that means "before; earlier; in front of." *The reporter waited in an anteroom until the politician could see her.* The prefix *anti-* means "against" or "opposed to." *Thousands of supporters turned out for the antipoverty rally.* Use *anti-* with a hyphen when it is followed by a capital letter (*anti-American*) or a word beginning with *i* (*anti-intellectual*). Otherwise, consult a dictionary.

anxious, eager. *Anxious* means "nervous," "troubled," or "worried." *The looming, dark clouds made Tim anxious. Eager* means "looking forward" and is often followed by the preposition *to. Stella was eager to receive the Christmas parcel.* Do not use *anxious* to mean "eager." *I'm eager* [not *anxious*] *to spend my gift certificate.*

anyone, any one. *Anyone* is an indefinite pronoun that means "any person at all." *Anyone* is singular. *Can anyone tell me what to do?* In *any one,* the pronoun *one* is preceded by the adjective *any.* Here the two words refer to any person or thing in a group. *Once the last of the patrons has left, you can jump into any one of the bumper cars.*

anyplace. *Anyplace* is informal for *anywhere.* Do not use *anyplace* in formal writing.

anyways, anywheres. *Anyways* and *anywheres* are non-standard for *anyway* and *anywhere,* respectively. Always use *anyway* and *anywhere* in formal speaking and writing.

as. Substituting *as* for *because*, *since*, and *while* may make a sentence vague or ambiguous. *Since* [not *as*] *we were stopping for gas, we decided to use the restroom.* If *as* were used in this sentence, the cause–effect relationship would be unclear.

as, like. See *like, as*.

averse, adverse. See *adverse, averse*.

awful, awfully. In formal English usage the adjective *awful* once meant "filled with awe" or "inspiring awe." Now, *awful* is more commonly used to mean "bad" or "terrible." *It was an awful day when I was fired.* The adverb *awfully* is sometimes used colloquially as an intensifier to mean "extremely" or "very." *He was awfully upset when he opened the bill.* Avoid such colloquial usage in formal writing.

awhile, a while. *Awhile* is an adverb. *Stay awhile, if you wish.* Use the article and noun, *a while*, as the object of a preposition. *We had obviously arrived too early, so we circled the block for a while.*

bad, badly. *Bad* is an adjective. *They felt bad about leaving the party early.* The word *badly* is an adverb. *His infected hand hurt badly.*

being as, being that. Both *being as* and *being that* are non-standard expressions used in place of the subordinate conjunctions *because* or *since*. *Since* [not *Being that*] *vandals had written on the walls, tough security measures were put in place.*

beside, besides. *Beside* is a preposition meaning "by the side of" or "next to." *Grass grows beside the stream.* *Besides* is an adverb meaning "moreover," or "furthermore." *Jeff did not want to fight; besides, he was injured.* *Besides* can also be a preposition meaning "in addition to," "except for," or "other than." *Besides me, there is no one working on the project.*

between, among. Use *among* when referring to relationships involving more than two people or things. *You can choose among fifteen sports.* Use *between* when referring to relationships involving two people or things. *When deciding which band is better, you need to take into account the difference in record sales between the two.*

bring, take. Use *bring* when something is being moved toward the speaker. *Please bring the thermometer to me.* Use *take* when something is being moved away. *I ask that you take the pizza to the Simpsons.*

burst, bursted; bust, busted. *Burst* is an irregular verb meaning "to fly apart suddenly with force; explode; break open." *The water-filled balloon burst when it hit the pavement.* *Bursted* is the non-standard past-tense form of *burst*; use the standard past tense (*burst*) instead. *Bust* and its past-tense form *busted* are slang.

can, may. *Can* means "know how to" or "be able to." *Mai-Ling can play the piano.* *May* means "be allowed to" or "have permission to." *Ted, you may go now.* The distinction in meaning between *can* and *may* is still made in formal writing. In informal English, *can* is widely used to mean "be able to" and "be allowed to."

capital, capitol. *Capital* refers to a city where the government of a country, province, or state is located. *Edmonton is the capital of Alberta. Capital* can also mean "the amount of money a company or person uses in carrying on a business." A *capitol* is a building in which American lawmakers meet. When referring to the building in which the U.S. Congress meets, capitalize the first letter, as in *Capitol.*

censor, censure. The verb *censor* means "to edit or remove from public view on moral or other grounds." *They will censor the violent movie before it can be seen in theatres.* The verb *censure* means "to express strong disapproval." *The House will censure the minister for giving misleading information.*

cite, site. The verb *cite* means "to quote, especially as an authority." *Doug cited the poet's use of allusion in his essay.* The noun *site* often means "a particular place." *The vacant field will be the site of a new shopping centre.*

climactic, climatic. *Climactic* is an adjective derived from *climax; climax* means "the highest point; point of highest interest; the most exciting part." *The scene in which the boy is reunited with his father is the climactic moment of the movie.* The adjective *climatic* means "of or having to do with climate." *In order for a tornado to occur, there must be certain climatic conditions.*

coarse, course. *Coarse* usually means "heavy and rough in texture" or "crude." *Shelley used a coarse sandpaper to finish the table. Course* means "a line of movement," "a direction taken," "a way, path, or track," or "a playing field." *Seeking help for your drinking problem is the right course of action.*

compare to, compare with. *Compare to* means "to represent as similar." *Shall I compare thee to a summer's day? Compare with* means "to point out how two persons or things are alike and how they differ." *I will compare Millay's poem with Eliot's.*

complement, compliment. The verb *complement* means "to reinforce, add to, or complete something." *The scarf complements his wardrobe.* As a noun, *complement* is something that completes. *Compliment* as a verb means "to say something in praise." *I must compliment you on your fine enunciation.* As a noun, *compliment* means "a remark of praise."

conscience, conscious. *Conscience* is a noun meaning "the sense of moral right and wrong." *His conscience would not let him shoplift the DVD. Conscious* is an adjective that means "aware; knowing." *Nancy Drew was conscious of a shadowy figure sneaking up behind her.*

consensus of opinion. *Consensus* means "general agreement." As a result, the phrase *consensus of opinion* is redundant. *A consensus* [not *consensus of opinion*] *is required before the motion will be passed.*

contact. *Contact* is often used informally as a verb meaning "to communicate with." In formal writing, use a precise verb such as *e-mail, telephone,* or *write. I will telephone* [not *contact*] *you for directions to the plant.*

continual, continuous. *Continual* means "repeated many times; very frequent." *When the roofers were here, there was continual hammering. Continuous* means "without a stop or a break." *During rush hour, there is a continuous line of cars.*

could care less. *Could care less* is non-standard and should not be used in formal writing. Use *couldn't care less* in its place. *Daphne couldn't care less how much the job pays, as long as it gives her satisfaction.*

could of. *Could of* is non-standard for *could have*. *If not for his injury, Mr. Martin could have [not could of] become a professional basketball player.*

council, counsel. *Council* is a noun used to describe "a group of people called together to talk things over, or give advice"; it also applies to "a group of people elected by citizens to make up laws." *A tribal council will decide the appropriate punishment.* A *councillor* is a member of the *council. Counsel* as a noun means "advice." *The chief gives wise counsel. Counsel* can also mean a lawyer. A *counsellor* is someone who gives advice or guidance.

course, coarse. See *coarse, course*.

criteria, criterion. *Criteria* are rules for making judgments. *Criteria* is the plural form of *criterion. The major criteria for the job are a background in multimedia and a readiness to work overtime.*

data, datum. *Data* are "facts or concepts presented in a form suitable for processing in order to draw conclusions." *Data* is the plural form of *datum*, which is rarely used. Increasingly *data* is used as a singular noun; however, careful writers use it as a plural. *The new data reveal [or, increasingly, reveals] that the economy is rebounding.*

defuse, diffuse. *Defuse* means "to take the fuse out" or "to disarm." *The counsellor managed to defuse the volatile family situation. Diffuse* as a verb means "to scatter" or "to spread out," but *diffuse* is more commonly used as an adjective to describe something spread out or, in the context of language, something wordy or verbose. *The smell of cologne diffused after we opened the windows. His speech was diffuse and did not focus on a particular point.*

delusion, allusion, illusion. See *allusion, illusion, delusion*.

differ from, differ with. *Differ from* means "to be unlike." *The brothers differ from each other only in their girlfriends. Differ with* means "to disagree with." *I used to differ with my stepmother on what time I should be home on Saturday night.*

different from, different than. In standard English the preferred form is *different from. The new edition of* Ulysses *is very different from the previous one.* However, *different than* is gaining wider acceptance, especially when *different from* creates an awkward construction. *He is a different person today than [as opposed to the more awkward from the person] he used to be.*

discreet, discrete. *Discreet* means "prudent and tactful in speech and behaviour." *The mayor was very discreet when talking about the manager's personal life.* Discrete means "separate; distinct." *There are discrete parts of the cell that perform specialized functions.*

disinterested, uninterested. *Disinterested* means "impartial." *The premier appointed a disinterested third party to mediate the dispute.* Uninterested means "lacking in interest," or "bored." *Shelley is uninterested in soap operas.*

don't. *Don't* is a contraction for *do not*. *Don't slam the door.* Do not use *don't* as a contraction for *does not*; the correct contraction is *doesn't*. *Selma doesn't [not don't] want to shovel the walk.*

due to. *Due to* means "caused by" or "owing to." It should be used as an adjective phrase following a form of the verb *to be*. *The inquest ruled that the death was due to driver error.* In formal writing, *due to* should not be used as a preposition meaning "because of." *Classes were cancelled because of [not due to] the heavy snowstorm.*

each. *Each* is singular.

eager, anxious. See *anxious, eager.*

effect, affect. See *affect, effect.*

e.g. This is the Latin abbreviation for *exempli gratia*, which means "for example." In formal writing, avoid *e.g.* and use phrases such as *for example* or *for instance* instead. *Many fish—for example, salmon and trout—will be affected.* (E.g. is always followed by a comma.)

either. *Either* is singular.

elicit, illicit. *Elicit* is a verb meaning "to draw forth" or "bring out." *Listening to a great symphony will elicit strong emotions.* The adjective illicit means "unlawful." *The neighbours had an illicit growing operation in their basement.*

elude, allude. See *allude, elude.*

emigrate from, immigrate to. *Emigrate* means "to leave one's own country or region and settle in another"; it requires the preposition *from*. *The Bhuttos emigrated from Pakistan.* Immigrate means "to enter and permanently settle in another country"; it requires the preposition *to*. *Mr. Bhutto's cousin now plans to immigrate to Canada.*

eminent, immanent, imminent. *Eminent* means "distinguished" or "exalted." *The eminent scientist delivered the lecture.* Immanent is an adjective that means "inherent" or "remaining within." *I believe most Canadians have an immanent goodness.* Imminent is an adjective meaning "likely to happen soon." *Given the troop movements, the general felt that an attack was imminent.*

enthused, enthusiastic. *Enthused* is sometimes informally used as an adjective meaning "having or showing enthusiasm." Use *enthusiastic* instead. *He becomes enthusiastic [not enthused] about Oilers playoff games.*

-ess. Many readers find the *-ess* suffix demeaning. Write *actor*, not *actress*; *singer*, not *songstress*; *poet*, not *poetess*.

etc. *Etc.* is an abbreviation that in English means "and other things." Do not use *etc.* to refer to people. In formal writing, it is preferable to use the expression *and so on* in place of *etc.* See also *and etc.*

eventually, ultimately. *Eventually* often means "an undefined time in the future." *Ultimately* commonly means "the greatest extreme or furthest extent." *Eventually* and *ultimately* are frequently used interchangeably. It is best to use *eventually* when referring to time and *ultimately* when referring to the greatest extent. *Eventually the robber will be found. I find it ultimately the most reasonable alternative.*

everybody, everyone. *Everybody* and *everyone* are both singular.

everyone, every one. *Everyone* is an indefinite pronoun meaning "every person." *Everyone wanted to purchase a ticket. Every one* is a pronoun, *one*, modified by an adjective, *every*; the two words mean "each person or thing in a group." *Every one* is frequently followed by *of*. *Every one of the merchants in Kamloops is participating in this promotion.*

except, accept. See *accept, except*.

except for the fact that. Avoid this wordy, awkward construction. Instead, use *except that*. *Alex would be a good candidate for office, except that he is unreliable.*

explicit, implicit. *Explicit* means "clearly expressed; directly stated." *The coach gave everyone but Keon explicit orders not to shoot. Implicit* means "meant but not clearly expressed or directly stated." *My mother-in-law's silence was implicit consent to pour her another glass of wine.*

farther, further. In formal English *farther* is used for physical distance. *On the map, Courtenay is farther than Ladysmith. Further* is used to mean "more" or "to a greater extent." *He took the teasing further than would be appropriate under any circumstances.*

female, male. *Female* and *male* are considered jargon if substituted for "woman" and "man." *Sixteen men* [not *males*] and *seventeen women* [not *females*] made the team.

fewer, less. Use *fewer* only to refer to numbers and things that can be counted. *There are fewer houses for sale than there were last year at this time.* Use *less* to refer to collective nouns or things that cannot be counted. *Generally, there is less traffic congestion at midday.*

finalize. *Finalize* is a verb meaning "to bring to a conclusion." The word, though often used, is considered jargon by many people. Use a clear, acceptable alternative. *The football coach completed* [not *finalized*] *plans for the game.*

flout, flaunt. *Flout* is a verb that means "to treat with contempt." *Magdalena flouted the rules of the road until she became one of the* *worst drivers in Canada. Flaunt* means "to show off." *Agnes flaunted her new MP3 player.*

flunk. *Flunk* is colloquial for *fail*, and it should be avoided in formal writing.

folks. *Folks* is informal for "one's family; one's relatives." In academic writing, use a more formal expression than *folks. My mother and father* [not *folks*] *are organizing the family reunion.*

fun. When used as an adjective, *fun* is colloquial; it should be avoided in formal writing. *The Jawbreaker was an exciting* [not *fun*] *ride.*

further, farther. See *farther, further.*

get. *Get* is a common verb with many slang and colloquial uses. Avoid the following uses of *get:* "to become" (*He got cold*); "to obtain revenge" (*Gillian got back at Ted for the rumours he spread*); "to annoy" (*His constant complaining finally got to me*); "to elicit an emotional response" (*The final scene in the movie really got to her*).

good, well. *Good* is an adjective. *Michael is a good skier. Well* is nearly always an adverb. *The racing team skis well.*

hanged, hung. *Hanged* is the past tense and past participle of *hang*, which means "to execute." *The man was convicted of treason and hanged. Hung* is the past tense and past participle of *hang*, which means "to fasten or be fastened to something." *Decorations for the dance hung from the ceiling.*

hardly. Avoid double negative expressions such as *not hardly* or *can't hardly. I can* [not *can't*] *hardly find words to express myself.*

has got, have got. Avoid using *have got* or *has got* when *have* or *has* alone will communicate the intended meaning. *I have* [not *have got*] *two more books to finish reading to complete the course requirements.*

he. Do not use only *he* when the complete meaning is "he or she." In modern usage, this is not inclusive. It is better to use *he or she* or pluralize the sentence to avoid a problem.

he/she, his/her. Use *he or she*, or *his or her* in formal writing.

hisself. Non-standard for *himself.*

hopefully. *Hopefully* is an adverb meaning "in a hopeful manner." *Hopefully* can modify a verb, an adjective, or another adverb. *They waited hopefully for news from the surgeon on how the operation had gone.* In formal writing, do not use *hopefully* as a sentence modifier with the meaning "I hope." *I hope* [not *Hopefully*] *the operation will be a success.*

hung, hanged. See *hanged, hung.*

i.e. The abbreviation *i.e.* stands for the Latin *id est*, which in English means "that is." In formal writing, use the English equivalent, *that is.* (*I.e.* is always followed by a comma.)

if, whether. *If* is used to express conditions. *If there is sufficient snow, we will go skiing at Whistler.* Use *whether* to express alternatives. *The couple was not sure whether to take the holiday in St. Lucia or in Aruba.*

illicit, elicit. See *elicit, illicit.*

illusion, allusion, delusion. See *allusion, illusion, delusion.*

immanent, imminent, eminent. See *eminent, immanent, imminent.*

immigrate to, emigrate from. See *emigrate from, immigrate to.*

immoral, amoral. See *amoral, immoral.*

implement. *Implement* means "to carry out." It is often unnecessary and pretentious. *The president carried out [not implemented] the board's recommendations.*

implicit, explicit. See *explicit, implicit.*

imply, infer. *Imply* means to "express indirectly." *Angie's grin implied that she knew Jo had a crush on Bono. Infer* means "to conclude by reasoning." *You could infer that the man was poor by his tattered clothes.*

in, into. *In* generally indicates a location or condition. *She is hiding in the house. Into* indicates a direction, a movement, or a change in condition. *He went into the house to look for her.*

individual. *Individual* is sometimes used as a pretentious substitute for *person*. *The person [not individual] sitting next to me slept through the entire play.*

ingenious, ingenuous. *Ingenious* means "clever" or "skillful." *The criminal devised an ingenious plan to rob the bank. Ingenuous* means "frank" and "simple." *His country manner was quite ingenuous.*

in regards to. *In regards to* confuses two phrases: *in regard to* and *as regards*. Use either one of these alternatives instead. *Talk to your counsellor in regard to the application.*

irregardless. *Irregardless* is non-standard English. Use *regardless* instead.

irritate, aggravate. See *aggravate, irritate.*

is when, is where. Do not use *when* or *where* following *is* in definitions. *Photosynthesis is the process by which [not is when] plant cells make sugar from carbon dioxide and water in the presence of chlorophyll and light.*

it is. *It is* becomes non-standard when used to mean "there is." *There is [not It is] a glowing disc in the night sky.*

its, it's. *Its* is a possessive pronoun. *The cat will come in its own good time. It's* is a contraction for *it is. It's the perfect time to buy a house.*

kind, kinds. *Kind* is singular and should not be treated as a plural. *This [not These] kind of painting was popular in that era. Kinds* is plural. *These kinds of paintings were popular in that era.*

kind of, sort of. *Kind of* and *sort of* are colloquial expressions meaning "rather" or "somewhat." Do not use these colloquialisms in formal writing. *I was somewhat [not kind of or sort of] disappointed by the low mark.*

lay, lie. See *lie, lay.*

lead, led. *Lead* is a soft heavy metal. *Led* is the past tense of the verb *lead*. *His accurate directions led me to the correct address.*

learn, teach. *Learn* means "to gain knowledge of or a skill by instruction, study, or experience." *I learned how to play chess. Teach* means "to impart knowledge or a skill." *I will teach [not learn] my little cousin to play the game.*

leave, let. *Leave* means "to go away." *Let* means "to allow or permit." Do not use *leave* with the non-standard meaning "to permit." *Let [not leave] me help you trim the fruit trees.*

led, lead. See *lead, led.*

less, fewer. See *fewer, less.*

liable. *Liable* means "legally responsible." Avoid using it to mean "likely." *Jeff will likely [not is liable to] catch many fish on this trip.*

licence, license. *Licence* is a noun meaning "legal permission by law to do something." *Joe's business licence hung prominently on the wall. License* is a verb meaning "to permit or authorize." *A veterinarian is licensed to practise animal medicine.*

lie, lay. *Lie* means "to recline." It is an intransitive verb, which means it does not take a direct object. The principal forms of the verb are *lie, lay,* and *lain. Lie down now. Lay* means "to put" or "to place." It is a transitive verb, which means it always requires a direct object. The principal parts of the verb are *lay, laid,* and *laid. Lay the guests' coats on the bed in the spare room.*

like, as. *Like* is a preposition, and it should be followed by a noun or a noun phrase. *Daniel looks like a million dollars. As* is a subordinating conjunction and should be used to introduce a dependent clause. *As I predicted, he is late again.*

loose, lose. *Loose* is an adjective meaning "not firmly fastened." *He has a loose tooth as a result of biting into the hard candy. Lose* is a verb meaning "to misplace" or "to be defeated." *He predicted that the Stampeders would lose the Grey Cup.*

lots, lots of. *Lots* and *lots of* are colloquial substitutes for *many, much,* and *a great deal.* They should not be used in formal writing.

male, female. See *female, male.*

mankind. *Mankind* is not an inclusive term, as it excludes women. Avoid it in favour of terms such as *humans, humanity, the human race,* or *humankind.*

may, can. See *can, may.*

may of, might of. *May of* and *might of* are non-standard English for *may have* and *might have*. *Mona might have [not might of] taken the chicken out of the oven too early.*

maybe, may be. *Maybe* is an adverb meaning "perhaps." *Maybe we should build the outdoor rink tomorrow. May be* is a verb phrase. *Since the temperature will be lower on Tuesday, that may be a better day.*

media, medium. *Media* is the plural of *medium. The media are offering too much coverage of sensational stories.*

moral, morale. *Moral* is a noun meaning "an ethical conclusion." *Morale* means "the attitude as regards courage, confidence, and enthusiasm." *Team morale was low after the twentieth defeat.*

most. When used to mean "almost," *most* is colloquial. This usage should be avoided in formal writing. *Almost [not Most] every student went to the party.*

must of. *Must of* is non-standard English for *must have*. See *may of, might of.*

myself. *Myself* is a reflexive pronoun. *I hurt myself. Myself* can also be an intensive pronoun. *I will go myself.* Do not use *myself* in place of *I* or *me. Jeremy and I [not myself] are going on a trip.*

neither. *Neither* is most often singular.

none. *None* is usually singular.

nowheres. *Nowheres* is non-standard English for *nowhere*.

number, amount. See *amount, number.*

of. *Of* is a preposition. Do not use it in place of the verb *have* after *could, should, would, may, must,* and *might. The Johnsons might have [not of] left their garage door open.*

off of. Omit *of* from the expression as *off* is sufficient. *The young boy fell off [not off of] the table.*

OK, O.K., okay. All three forms are acceptable in informal writing and speech. However, avoid these colloquial expressions in formal writing and speech.

parameters. *Parameter* is a mathematical term that means "a quantity that is constant in a particular calculation or case but varies in other cases." It is sometimes used as jargon to mean any limiting or defining element or feature. Avoid such jargon and use precise English instead. *The whole project had very vague guidelines [not parameters].*

passed, past. *Passed* is the past tense of the verb *pass,* which means "to go by." *Uncle Theo passed by our front window.* Never use *past* as a verb. *Past* can be an adjective that means "gone by; over." *They overcame their past misunderstanding. Past* can also be a noun meaning "the time before the present." *Canada has a rich and glorious past.* Finally, *past* can be a preposition. *Past the exit on the highway, there was a service station.*

people, persons. Use *people* to refer to a group of individuals who are anonymous and uncounted. *The people of South Africa have a long history of apartheid.* Generally, you may use *persons* or *people* when referring to a countable number of individuals. *Only five persons [or people] attended the town meeting.*

percent, per cent, percentage. Always use *percent* (also spelled *per cent*) with specific numbers. *The survey revealed that 48 percent of Canadians want their country to become a republic. Percentage* means "part of" or "portion," and it is used when no number is provided. *A large percentage of the population favoured the Liberals.*

phenomenon, phenomena. *Phenomenon* means "a fact, event or circumstance that can be observed." *Phenomena* is the plural of *phenomenon. There were all sorts of paranormal phenomena taking place in the haunted house.*

plus. *Plus* is a non-standard substitute for *and.* Do not use *plus* to join independent clauses. *He has a driver's licence; however [not plus], it has expired.*

p.m. See *a.m., p.m.*

pore, pour. *Pore* is an intransitive verb meaning "to read or study carefully" or "to ponder." *Ahmed has been poring over his chemistry notes to prepare for his exam. Pour* means "to cause to flow in a stream." *It has been pouring rain for days.*

practice, practise. *Practice* is a noun meaning "an action done several times over to gain a skill." *Practice will improve your dribbling. Practise* is a verb meaning "to do something again and again in order to learn it." *Su Li practises the violin twice a day.* In American spelling, both the noun and verb are spelled *practice.*

precede, proceed. *Precede* means "to go or come before." *A mild gust preceded the hurricane. Proceed* means "to go on after having stopped" or "to move forward." *After a family meeting about finances, we proceeded with the wedding plans.*

principal, principle. The noun *principal* means "a chief person" or "a sum of money that has been borrowed." *After Mr. Toutant's retirement from Dauphin Elementary School, a new principal was appointed.* The noun *principle* means "a fact or belief on which other ideas are based." *The constitution is based on the principles of equality and justice.* Note, too, that *principal* can be an adjective, meaning "main." *The principal reason I didn't vote was my disagreement with all the candidates' platforms.*

proceed, precede. See *precede, proceed.*

quote, quotation. *Quote* is a verb meaning "to repeat the exact words of." *She quoted the precise line from "Leda and the Swan" to illustrate her point. Quotation* is a noun meaning "a passage quoted." Do not use *quote* as a shortened form of *quotation. Using a relevant quotation [not quote] is often a good way to begin a speech.*

raise, rise. *Raise* means "to move to a higher level; to elevate." It is a transitive verb, which means it requires a direct object. *The stage manager raised the curtain. Rise* means "to go up." It is an intransitive verb, which means it does not require a direct object. *The smoke rises.*

real, really. *Real* is an adjective. Occasionally, in informal speech and writing, it is used as an adverb, but this usage should be avoided in formal writing. *Really* is an adverb. *Don was really [not real] excited.* In informal writing and speech, *real* and *really* are used as intensifiers to mean "extremely" or "very"; such usage should be avoided in formal writing and speech.

reason is because. *Reason is because* is a redundant expression. Use *reason is that* instead. *One reason we moved from Moose Jaw is that [not is because] Mom got a teaching job at a community college.*

reason why. *Reason why* is a redundant expression. In its place use either *reason* or *why. I still do not know why [not the reason why] she rejected my invitation.*

regretfully, regrettably. *Regretfully* means "full of regret." It describes a person's attitude of regret. *Regretfully, he wrote to apologize. Regrettably* means that circumstances are regrettable. *Regrettably, the circus was rained out today.*

rein/reign. *Rein* refers to the restraint a driver uses to control an animal or any kind of restraint in general. *The equestrian champion reined in his horse forcefully. Reign* means "royal authority." *Shakespeare wrote* Hamlet *during the reign of James I.* Be careful not to confuse them in certain idiomatic phrases, such as "give free rein [not reign] to."

relation, relationship. *Relation* is used to describe the association between two or more things. *The scientist studied the relation between lung cancer and smog. Relationship* is used to describe the association or connection between people. *Peter and Olga had a professional relationship that soon blossomed into a personal one.*

respectfully, respectively. *Respectfully* is an adverb meaning "showing or marked by proper respect." *She respectfully presented her counterargument in the debate. Respectively* is an adverb meaning "singly in the order designated or mentioned." *Chand, Doug, and Lenore are a plastic surgeon, bus driver, and company vice-president respectively.*

rise, raise. See *raise, rise.*

sensual, sensuous. *Sensual* is an adjective meaning "relating to gratification of the physical senses." *The chef obtains sensual pleasure from cooking. Sensuous* is an adjective meaning "pleasing to the senses." *Sensuous* is always favourable and often applies to the appreciation of nature, art, or music. *She obtains a sensuous delight from Mozart's music.*

set, sit. *Set* means "to put in place or put down, or to position." It is a transitive verb, requiring a direct object, and its principal parts are *set, set, set. Ali set the book on the ledge. Sit* means "to be seated." It is an intransitive verb, not requiring a direct object, and its principal parts are *sit, sat, sat. Set* is sometimes a non-standard substitute for *sit.* Avoid this usage in formal writing. *The dog sat* [not *set*] *down.*

shall, will. *Shall* was once used with the first-person singular and plural as the helping verb with future-tense verbs. *I shall visit my grandfather on Wednesday. We shall deliver the results on Thursday.* In modern usage *will* has replaced *shall. I will see you on Friday.* The word *shall* is still often used in polite questions. *Shall I bring the newspaper to your door?*

she/he, her/his. See *he/she, his/her.*

should of. *Should of* is non-standard for *should have. He should have* [not *should of*] *submitted the essay on time.*

since. *Since* should mainly be used in situations describing time. *We have been waiting for the bus since midnight.* Do not use *since* as a substitute for *because* in cases where there is any chance of confusion. *Since we lost the division, we have been playing our second-string players.* Here *since* could mean "from that point in time" or "because."

sit, set. See *set, sit.*

site, cite. See *cite, site.*

somebody, someone. *Somebody* and *someone* are singular.

something. *Something* is singular.

sometime, some time, sometimes. *Sometime* is an adverb meaning "at an indefinite or unstated time." *Let's meet sometime on Thursday.* In *some time* the adjective *some* modifies the noun *time. We haven't seen the Jebsons for some time. Sometimes* is an adverb meaning "at times; now and then." *Sometimes I'm not sure what major to pursue.*

sort of, kind of. See *kind of, sort of.*

sneaked, snuck. *Sneaked* is the correct past participle. *Sameer sneaked* [not *snuck*] *into his parents' closet looking for his birthday presents.*

stationary, stationery. *Stationary* means "not moving." *At the club, he rode on a stationary bike. Stationery* refers to paper and other writing products. *I will need to buy the stationery at the business supply store.*

suppose to, use to. See *use to, suppose to.*

sure and. *Sure and* is non-standard. Instead, use *sure to. Please be sure to* [not *sure and*] *edit your work carefully.*

take, bring. See *bring, take.*

teach, learn. See *learn, teach.*

than, then. *Than* is a conjunction used to make comparisons. *I would rather have cheesecake than pie. Then* is an adverb used to indicate past or future time. *My husband will do the vacuuming, and then he will wax the floors.*

that, who. See *who, which, that.*

that, which. Most North American writers use *that* for restrictive clauses and *which* for non-restrictive clauses. Note, however, that in some circles *that* and *which* are increasingly treated as grammatically identical. Most grammar checkers still distinguish between them. Your instructor may or may not observe this distinction.

theirselves. *Theirselves* is non-standard English for *themselves. They amused themselves* [not *theirselves*] *by going to the drive-in.*

them. *Them* is non-standard when it is used in place of *those. Please place those* [not *them*] *flowers on the kitchen table.*

then, than. See *than, then.*

there, their, they're. *There* is an adverb meaning "at or in that place." *I'll call home when I get there. There* can also be an expletive, a phrase at the beginning of a clause. *There are two beautiful dogs in the garage. Their* is a possessive pronoun. *It was their first house. They're* is a contraction for *they are. They're first in line for tickets.*

this kind. See *kind, kinds.*

thru. *Thru* is a colloquial spelling of *through*. Do not use *thru* in formal academic or business writing.

to, too, two. *To* can be a preposition. *They swayed to the rhythm. To* can also be part of an infinitive. *We need to talk. Too* is an adverb. *There are too many people in the city. Two* is a number. *I have two red pens.*

toward, towards. Both versions are acceptable; however, *toward* is preferred in Canadian English.

try and. *Try and* is non-standard English. Instead use *try to. Try to* [not *Try and*] *be polite.*

ultimately, eventually. See *eventually, ultimately.*

uninterested, disinterested. See *disinterested, uninterested.*

unique. Like *straight, round,* and *complete, unique* is an absolute. There are not degrees of uniqueness. Especially in formal writing, avoid expressions such as *more unique* and *most unique.*

usage, use. *Usage* refers to conventions, most often of language. *Placing "ain't" in a sentence is non-standard usage. Use* means "to employ." Do not substitute *usage* when *use* is required. *I do not think surfing the Internet is the proper use* [not *usage*] *of your study time.*

use to, suppose to. *Use to* and *suppose to* are non-standard for *used to* and *supposed to. We used to* [not *use to*] *have roast beef for dinner every Sunday night.*

utilize. *Utilize* means "to put to use." Often *use* can be substituted, as *utilize* can make writing sound pretentious. *He will use [not utilize] the best material to tile the bathroom.*

wait for, wait on. *Wait for* means "to await." *The girls are waiting for the commuter train. Wait on* means "to serve." It should not be used as substitute for *wait for. The owner of the bistro waited on our table.*

ways. *Ways* is colloquial in usage when designating distance. *Edmonton is quite a way [not ways] from Vancouver.*

weather, whether. *Weather* is a noun describing "the state of the atmosphere at a given time and place." *The weather in central Canada has been unseasonably warm. Whether* is a conjunction that signals a choice between or among alternatives. *Grif did not know whether to stay or to go.*

well, good. See *good, well.*

where. *Where* is non-standard in usage when it is substituted for *that* as a subordinate conjunction. *I read in the newspaper that [not where] Arundhati Roy will be giving a reading at the university.*

whether, if. See *if, whether.*

which. See *that, which* and *who, which, that.*

while. Do not use *while* as a substitute for "although" or "whereas" if such usage risks ambiguity. *Although [not While] Jennifer's grades got worse, Jack's got better.* If *while* were used, it could mean "although" or "at the same time."

who, which, that. Use *who*, not *which*, to refer to persons. Most often *that* is used to refer to things. *There is the boy who [not that] took the candies.* However, *that* may be used to refer to a class or group of people. *The team that scores the most points wins.*

who, whom. *Who* is used for subjects and subject complements. *Who is coming to dinner? Whom* is used for objects. *He did not know whom to ask.*

who's, whose. *Who's* is a contraction for *who is. Who's going to the dinner? Whose* is a possessive pronoun. *Whose life is it anyway?*

will, shall. See *shall, will.*

would of. *Would of* is non-standard English for *would have. He would have [not would of] achieved a perfect score if he had obtained one more strike.*

you. Avoid using *you* in an indefinite sentence to mean "anyone." *Any collector [not You] could identify it as a fake.*

your, you're. *Your* is a possessive pronoun. *Your bicycle is in the garage. You're* is a contraction for *you are. You're the first person I contacted about the job.*

INDEX
index

" If you don't find it in
the index, look very carefully
through the entire catalogue. "

— SEARS, ROEBUCK, AND CO.,
CONSUMERS GUIDE, 1897

in Columbia Online style, 179–
80, 182–83
in CSE style, 176–78,
179–80, 183
of electronic sources, 119–20,
145–46, 179–80, 182–83
in MLA style, 114–20
of multiple works, 118, 124–25,
145
of print sources, 116–18, 143–45
including/included, 83
independent clauses, 4, 9, 81
punctuation with, 72, 80–81, 82
individual, 203
infinitives, 20, 37–38
infinitive phrases, 38, 39
ingenious, ingenuous, 203
interjections, 78
interrogative tags, 78
interviews, 135–36, 145, 171
introductions, 126
irregardless, 203
irritate, 195
is because, 45–46
is when, is where, 45–46, 203
it, 15–16
it is, 28, 203
its, it's, 86, 109, 203
items
paired, 47–49, 98
in series, 46–47, 73–74, 96

jargon, 56–57
journals. *See also* periodicals
articles in, 127, 131, 150, 179,
189
online, 131, 151–52, 168–69

kind, kinds, 203
kind of, 204

language
emotional, 64–65
inclusive, 12, 62
nonsexist, 62–63
precision in, 64
pretentious, 58
lay, 204
lead, led, 204
learn, 204
leave, let, 204

lectures, 133
less, 201
letters (alphabet), 85
letters (correspondence)
citing, 128, 136, 145, 151, 169
to editor, 128, 151
salutation for, 82
liable, 204
licence, license, 204
lie, 204
like, 204
lists, 6, 82, 95. *See also* discussion
lists; series
literary works, 117–18
location information. *See* page
references
loose, lose, 109, 204
lots, 204

magazines. *See also* periodicals
articles in, 126–28, 131, 167,
188
online, 131
publication information, 147
mailing lists. *See* discussion lists;
forums
male, 201
mankind, 204
maps, 136
may, 205
may of, 205
maybe, may be, 205
measurement, units of, 28, 107
mechanics (of writing), 100–111
media, medium, 205
memos, 145
metaphors, 70
might of, 205
mixed constructions, 43–46
MLA style documentation, 114–42
format, 120–21, 137–42
in-text citations, 114–20
notes, 137
sample paper, 139–42
works cited list, 120–36
Modern Languages Association,
129. *See also* MLA style documentation
modifiers, 75
problems with, 24–25, 35–39
mood, 41–42